My Family Quilt

by Violetta Elrod

Copyright © 2017 by Violetta Elrod

All rights reserved.

ISBN 978-1-62806-168-0

Library of Congress Control Number 2018942784

Published by Salt Water Media
29 Broad Street, Suite 104
Berlin, MD 21811
www.saltwatermedia.com

Cover design courtesy of Andrea Berg

Cover photograph and interior illustration provided by the author, Violetta Elrod.

Acknowledgements:

The following stories were told to me by my grandparents, their family, and friends after I came into the Ruark family.

I feel it is necessary to say also I used a few fictional names to protect the innocent as well as the guilty.

I have done my best to tell our family stories as accurately as my memory allows me to.

Dedication:

There are so many people I want to thank for helping me write our Ruark family's history. The following stories are an accumulation of stories told to me by my grandparents, their family members, and their friends. I wish to thank everyone for sharing your special memories with me.

I would be remiss if I did not include my four children, my brother, my three granddaughters, and even my precious great-grandbabies. Our family has carried on the tradition of sharing their memories whenever we get together. I have gotten used to their "Don't forget the time..." When I believed I was finally finished, one particular person would always say, "You forgot to include the time when..." So my memories have grown enough to fill more books for you to enjoy. As my grandfather would often remark, "Some memories were bad, but most were good."

Ann Shaheen volunteered to proofread my beginning efforts and her comment I shall always treasure was, "Some parts made me laugh and some parts made me cry!"

Last but certainly not the least, I want to thank Stephanie Fowler, my editor and publisher of Salt Water Media for all of her kindness, encouragement, and patience.

*The more he heard, the less he spoke;
the less he spoke, the more he learned!*

Author's Note

A quilt is like a blanket made by "piecing" or sewing scraps of various pieces of material together. The pieces could be rayon, cotton, silk, polyester, burlap, or whatever you chose.

Those small pieces of material might come from clothes which had been worn at various times in someone's life. They may be from your great-grandfather's everyday work shirt, your grandmother's wedding dress, your mother's prom gown, your own christening set, or maybe a piece from the outfit your baby wore home from the hospital. The choices were yours.

These material scraps of memories were gathered over time until some family member sewed them all together with ribbons and trims collected and kept over the years from various memorial occasions like Christmas, Easter, Halloween, weddings, birthdays or other festive times. When all of these gathering and saving pieces were sewn together the result would be a beautiful quilt to wrap you in a comforting embrace and keep you secure and warm on the coldest nights.

My life has been like a colorful quilt which began with these memories of my grandfather, Lee Bahnum Ruark, who was born in 1867. I was not born untill 1932 and would not have been able to write this book when it first began. Fortunately I obtained many of these memories from my grandparents, their family members, and their friends. The following stories based on those memory scraps were given to me by all of them. I want to thank everyone for sharing your special memories with me. I have saved and pieced them together here for you to enjoy. Turn the page, get comfortable as I share the Ruark family quilts with you.

- Violetta Elrod

Read on and enjoy!

Chapter 1 - Lee Bahnum Ruark

Everyone who knew Lee loved and respected him and only had good things to say about him. I learned a handshake from him was his bond and would seal any bargain or agreement he made. His word was better and more binding than any legal document ever written on paper by some fancy lawyer from up the road. One of his friends, Seth Parker, loved to tell everyone about the time Lee went to do some banking business: "The bank president was a fella who was not very old. In fact he didn't even look like he was shaving yet. He was audacious enough to ask Lee for a reference. Well Lee just rose up out of his chair and told that young whupper snapper, 'If you want to see my reference young fellow you just look square in my eyes. That's my reference!'" Laughing loudly, Seth would add, "And Lee got his money too!"

Lee loved his whiskey, his women, his fiddle, his coon-hunting hound dog, his land, and his God. He was a tall, handsome, redheaded Irishman with the most stylishly waxed and best-kept handle-bar mustache around. His smile, loud laughter, free spirit, and twinkling blue eyes caused many young ladies in Salisbury to dream of becoming Mrs. Lee Bahnum Ruark. However he was not a rich man. Therefore the parents of those young girls did not consider him a good catch. So Lee enjoyed his life in the country to the fullest and remained a carefree bachelor for quite a while. He felt he had every thing he needed in life. He had his good health, owned a small piece of property, and his stubborn contrary ole mule, Sully, to plow his land. He said he had named her Sully because she was so sullen. Lee loved to joke about her and say, "Sully's a pretty good worker after I get her attention with a sturdy 2 by 4 piece of wood!"

Lee was never lonesome for company. He had many interesting conversations with his pigs, his chickens, and his cows. Lee's horse, Major, was the most beautiful and fastest horse in the whole town. Probably the whole county, since it seemed as though everyone around wanted to buy him. But no matter how high the offer Lee would just smile and shake his head, "Nope!" He would never sell his good friend. Major was very dependable and would never leave him stranded. Lee and his town buddies would often get to visiting and become engaged in some serious talking about girls or politics. Sometimes the demijohns would be swapped around more than usual. When this happened he would become just a bit tipsy and unable to navigate his feet. So he'd just stumble onto his buckboard and Major would carry him directly home. His faithful friend would wait through the night for him to wake and greet the day with mumbling about his aching head and grumbling, "I guess I just stayed out too late!"

Chapter 2 – The Coon Hunt

One of Lee's most prized possessions was his ole coon-hunting hound dog named Blue. Every year at coon hunting season Lee and most of his male friends got their hunting dogs and guns out and went to hunt some raccoons. Far from the noise in Salisbury, in the woods they all loved, there would be a slight touch of frost in the air. The night would be very still and quiet. A huge full moon would shine down on the men. They used this bright light to help them keep up with their dogs when the run started. While the men waited for the dogs to catch the scent of a coon they would huddle around their warm fire swapping their stories and their whiskey. Their dogs had all been trained to be silent and still. The people in Salisbury could always tell when the men got serious and let their dogs off the leash to do some real coon hunting. Then the barking, baying, and howling of the hounds could be heard for miles. They were off and running with the excited hunters trying to keep up through briars, mud holes, and over tree stumps. There were times when the bright moon would hide behind the clouds for a few moments. Then there would be curses of all kinds as the men fell and stumbled into trees, water, and rocks. But they'd crawl up and try to stay with their dogs for the finish.

A kind man might mercifully shoot the old coon dead and quickly put it out of misery. But usually after the exciting chase the dogs' loud barking terrified the poor creature who managed to quickly scramble to safety up a tall tree. This was the grandest moment of the night. The dogs circled the tree and increased their loud howling. A bad decision was often made at this time by the coon. He would make a last desperate attempt to live. The poor thing would jump from the tree and again try to outrun those dogs. But they would just rush and tear him or her apart. Laughing loudly one of the men shouted, "I hope those hounds leave enough fur to make a good coon skin hat for one of us!" Hooting and hollering the men would return to their campfire, laughing loudly over the exciting moments of the night. They would gather up their dogs, guns, and empty bottles and stagger home in the early morning light with tales to tell and retell until their next great coon hunt.

Chapter 3 – Bachelor Days

Lee really enjoyed his bachelor days. He plowed, planted and harvested his crops. He fed his pigs, his cows, and his chickens. He butchered his hogs, milked his cows, and gathered his eggs. Occasionally he rode into Salisbury when it was absolutely necessary. After getting all of his necessities at the general store he would stroll down to the center of Salisbury where everyone usually gathered. There he flirted, danced, and played his fiddle for himself and his friends well into the night hours. But when the girls got too close he always flew home like a rabbit in the bushes.

Lee never talked too much about religion. But as he worked he always seemed to be muttering or talking to himself. When I was older I learned he was actually talking to his God out in the fields, far from his family and rascally friends. You could often hear him loudly singing the old hymns he had learned at his mother's knee. He knew he was not one of the best singers around. There were times when he would laugh and make excuses for his booming off key renditions by saying, "I believe my Good Book and it just says you should make a joyful noise unto the Lord and by cracky I reckon that's exactly what I'm doing!" Whenever he found himself confined indoors because of severe weather he loved to kick back in front of his huge fireplace and sing joyfully in his loud boisterous voice. Some of the words to his winter tunes were a bit wild and his nearby neighbors enjoyed them especially when he accompanied himself on his fiddle.

Chapter 4 – The Seasons

Lee loved all the seasons of the year. In the spring after getting his crops in the ground he often planted a few flowers just for his own pleasure. At times he might pick a few of them for a pretty young lady who had caught his eye.

Summer was time for great fun. He had homemade signs all along his property lines clearly warning, "Trespass onto my property and you'll get shot!" Everyone knew he was a man of his word and they steered clear. If an emergency ever occurred when he might really be needed folks could just leave a note on his front door, knock gently, and leave quickly and quietly. He felt quite safe when he peeled off his winter woolies and jumped into his private swimming hole when it was well past the time of freezing. Old Blue, his coon hunting dog, would jump in with him. Blue didn't seem to mind Lee was buck naked as the day he was born.

Fall brought hard work and long days. But it was also a fun season for Lee. When the green leaves began to change colors to their brilliant shades of red, orange, and yellow and when the little squirrels started storing up their food for the winter Lee began to do the same. It was time to butcher one of his cows. Half of the cow would supply him with meat to eat through the cold winter. The other half would be taken to town to be traded for things such as flour, salt, molasses, sugar, coffee and other necessary things like his Johnny Walker and his winter supply of snuff which he called his "Chawin' Terbacky." He would spare his second cow. She would supply fresh milk to drink. The hog he would butcher and cut up into smaller portions. He would then hang it in his smoke house where it would cook slowly. Then it would be ready to eat about the time ole man winter showed up. His chickens would provide him with fresh eggs to go with his bacon or ham and some homemade biscuits.

When winter was on the way Lee would stack a huge pile of

firewood next to his fireplace and prepare for any snow or cold weather which might come along. He prayed it would not snow this year like it did in the old days when he was a lot younger. He remembered how the snow would fall at times and be six feet or more high. He loved to tell about the time Johnson's Lake in Salisbury froze so hard and thick. Lee explained he was a grown man then. But he was still young and foolish and he warned any young boys who were listening not to take the same dare he did. Some one had dared him to walk across the ice to the shore on the other side of the lake. Lee just scoffed, "Heh, I'll not only walk over it! I'll drive Major pulling a load of wood across it too!" And he did!

In the old days it sometimes snowed so hard it would become a real blizzard. Then Lee would not be able to see his hand in front of his face. But his animals out in the barn needed food and water. His solution to this problem was to tie a long strong rope to his back porch post and the other end around his waist. This was done so he would not wander from the path and get lost in the snow. When he finished his chores he would just follow the rope back to his nice warm house. Sometimes, for a special treat at dinner, he would use the rope and porch post to go down to his frozen creek and cut some ice to put in his cup of milk. He also really enjoyed scooping up a pail of freshly fallen snow, adding some crushed vanilla beans, some sugar, with a bit of molasses, and he'd have the best snow cream on the shore.

Lee always felt so contented in the winter. He had plenty of good food stored in his pantry, a few bottles of his precious Johnny Walker whiskey, and he had his fiddle for entertainment. Lee said he liked having his dog, Ole Blue, to talk with because he was always agreeable and never interrupted him in the middle of their talks. On cool nights Lee would lay an ole brick on his logs in his fireplace to get it good and hot. He'd wrap it up in a rag and then put it under his quilts to keep his feet nice and toasty.

If it got especially cold his faithful companion, Blue, would curl up at the foot of his bed and keep him even warmer. Lee called this a one dog night. At times though it got so cold it was what Lee called a three dog night. Then he'd laugh and say, "I sure wish I had a couple more dogs to pull up for covers."

To keep himself occupied and to prevent any winter doldrums Lee invented an amusing game for the long winter season. He would roll a pinch of snuff around in his mouth. You weren't ever supposed to swallow any of it. When it was ready to spit he would aim for the empty can he had placed as a target on the floor in front of his ole rocking chair. If the tarry juice went into the can he would give out a loud, "Yah Whooo!" and move the can further away. If he missed the can there'd be an even louder, "Damn!" With a low grumble he'd try it again and again until he got it in the can. His rough hewn floor was spattered with the black gummy record of his many misses. When he tired of this game or playing his fiddle he would just wrap up nice and warm in his old bear skin, sit by the roaring fire, and sip his delicious store-bought coffee which he liked strong and black. His friends swore his coffee was so strong a spoon could stand on the top of it and not sink to the bottom.

He often leaned back in his old rocker and thought to himself, "*There ain't nothing more a man could wish for.*" Then he would close his eyes, drift off to sleep, and dream about the coming spring.

Chapter 5 – Lee's Trespasser

Spring came at last with warm sunshine and birds who were chirping noisily in the trees. Believing he was alone Lee stepped out of his long johns and strolled out onto his porch to smell the sweet fresh air of the new spring and take a really big stretch. He was surprised to see his nearest neighbor, Seth Parker, sitting quietly in his rocker on the front porch. Lee bellered, "Boy, can't you read my signs? Those words mean to keep the hell away or you could be dead!" Seth jumped up from the rocker as if he had been struck by lightning or worse was going to be shot by Lee. Seeing the scared look on Seth's face, Lee laughed loudly and Seth joined in, "I knew those signs meant every one 'cept me!"

Seth was all decked out in his Sunday-go-to-meeting best. They neither one remarked or even seemed to be aware of the fact Lee was standing there naked on his porch in broad day light wearing nothing but his birthday suit!

Seth was quick to remind Lee about the church social in town. It had been a long lonely winter for Seth. He was anxious to get started. It was about two miles to town and he really didn't want to walk that far. He was hoping Lee would give him a ride in his buckboard. Lee showed little interest in Seth's enthusiasm for the church social. He usually avoided most of Salisbury's happenings. He didn't like what he called a bunch of poor folks strutting around in their Sunday clothes like a bunch of bright-colored, brainless peacocks showing off their gaudy feathers. So Seth began talking about all those pretty young girls who would be there. Lee still showed no interest. Seth continued on and reminded Lee those girls had baskets of delicious home cooked food just waiting for some handsome young man like Lee to bid on.

Seth rambled on, "Don't you remember Lee? The church has these money raisers every Spring on the first of April and usually a lot of money is collected. This year they are aiming to get enough money to put up a bell in the new church steeple. The lucky fellow who bids the highest amount of money on a girl's basket will win the basket of food and the all day company of the young lady who cooked the food and owned the basket. Then if you both enjoy the day's company you'd be able to take her to the big dance in the moonlight downtown in Salisbury. That lucky feller could be you Lee!"

Seth was hunting for a bride and kept it no secret. He snickered and added, "Maybe I'll get lucky this year and since nature will take its course there will be quite a few weddings in the month of April. Then a whole bunch of babies should start coming on the following January." Lee thought Seth was a nice enough fellow. But he could not understand why he was so anxious to get a wife and then have to raise a whole bunch of children.

Seth had often tried to explain why to Lee but he was always unsuccessful. So he tried again, "Lee, you know I grew up in a big family. I had four sisters and seven brothers and of course my mother and father. Now I've moved way out here in the country all by myself. I'm just powerful lonely. You are the only man I can call a real friend. I don't even have an old dog like your Blue to keep my feet warm on cold winter nights! I want a bunch of younguns because after they have grown to some size I can just sit on my porch and watch them do my work for me!"

Being a contented bachelor Lee still didn't get it. Seth's last pitch about brides and babies didn't interest him at all since he was very happy living alone. He didn't need anybody especially some strong-willed woman telling him what, where, and how to do something. He was definitely not hunting for any bride!

Lee reasoned silently, *"It's been a long cold winter and I do need my supplies to get my crops planted. The home cooked food sure sounds mighty tempting and the money raised is for the Lord's house.*" He dashed in to get a little more presentable. When he came out wearing his newest shirt, best coveralls, and of course his ever present straw hat, Seth was hitching Major to Lee's buckboard. "Wull now, don't you look just like a real peacock?"

Seth laughed, "But you forgot something. You can't go without your fiddle! You never know you might find a use for it."

Lee dashed back inside. He gave his shoes a lick and a promise with the dish rag and grabbed his fiddle. When he came out this time, clutching his fiddle case, he was hot to trot! Seth was already sitting on Lee's wagon on the driver's seat ready to go.

Chapter 6 – The Church Social

Seth kept rambling on but Lee was lost in his own thoughts and paid no attention to him at all.

He was thinking what a perfect day this was. The wild flowers were blooming. The birds were chirping. "*Yep,*" Lee thought, "*God's in his heaven and everything is right with the world. There ain't any thing more needed to make this day a bit better!*" He whispered a silent prayer thanking the good Lord for his health and all his blessings.

Seth interrupted Lee's thoughts by yelling, "There they are! Ain't they the prettiest girls you've ever seen? And each one has a big basket of the tastiest food you've ever put in your mouth. Come on Major don't let us down now. Just keep on high stepping old boy! When those pretty girls see us riding up with you they will give us their full attention!"

Lee gave his little cough and said to Seth, "Now boy, don't go getting too excited. Hunting a girl is kind of like fishing. You have to stay in control. Show them your bait and wait patiently until you've got them on your hook. Then reel them in quick before they know what's happened!"

"Well," laughed Seth. "I never could manage to catch any fish! But I'm going to take your advice and maybe I'll get lucky this year with one of those girls."

Lee cautioned Seth, "Just remember now. The secret is to be calm and patient and let them come to you! Act like you are not interested at all! Now let's go our separate ways and see who gets lucky first!" Seth raced off like an excited schoolboy while Lee sat down under a nearby tree and looked like he was just relaxing.

He was totally relaxed until he noticed the most beautiful lady he had ever seen and she was strolling straight toward him. He started to rise up to greet her. She seemed not to even notice him and just kept walking on by. Lee was caught completely off guard and didn't know why she had failed to see him. None of the young girls from Salisbury had ever ignored him before.

Seth walked by with a pretty little girl on his arm and he was "smilin just like a possum chewing on a yellow jacket!" All this did not sit well with Lee. He thought he would surely land his prize before Seth. Lee rationalized silently, *"It could be this little lady has a kind of a seeing problem and is too proud or too poor to wear glasses. Maybe I ought to just stroll past and give her a hello. Yep, that's just what I'll do!"*

Lee strolled right in front of her. He gave her his very best smile and spoke, "How do. It's a lovely day ain't it?"

"Yes indeed!" she laughed and continued with her walk.

"What in tarnation is wrong? Can't she see I'm interested in her?" Lee was so annoyed he almost threw his hat on the ground. But he kept it on his head and approached her again. "That's a mighty big basket of food you're carrying Missy. I'd be much obliged if you'd allow me to carry it for you."

"Oh," she smiled, "This isn't really too heavy. I'm used to working hard and carrying things much heavier. I do appreciate you asking me though."

"I insist!" Lee almost shouted as he grabbed the basket from her arm.

She smiled again, "Well, I really can't say no to such a well mannered man as you." Lee was totally bewildered by her indifferent behavior. He just could not understand her. After their introductions they spent the whole day trying to figure each other out. He made an outrageous high bid on her basket. When he glared at the other men they knew he meant for them to stop their bidding. No one dared out bid him because his look plainly told them he wanted this young lady at least for the day.

Lee and Sarah enjoyed the picnic, their afternoon together,

and dancing under the stars in downtown Salisbury during the night. Years later they both laughed about their first meeting. Lee said Sarah must have heard what he said to Seth. "She just stayed calm and seemed not to be interested in me at all. I took her bait hook, line, and sinker!"

Like any married couple, Lee and Sarah had their differences over the years but their friends and neighbors were not aware of those times. Mr. and Mrs. Ruark's marriage was thought to be one made in heaven and was held up as an example to every young couple thinking about getting married.

Chapter 7 – Ruark Children

The normal number of children in a family on a farm in those days was always hoped to be twelve or more. There were two sayings well understood by country people, 'From sun up to sun down there's much work to be done.' and 'The more hands the better!' Both Lee and Sarah wanted to have the expected number of twelve children in their Ruark family tree.

Unfortunately only eight Ruark babies survived. They were Carey, Elmer, Johnny, Roy, Edna, Afrey, Fred, and last but certainly not the least was Emma.

Carey had helped raise her three younger brothers. Lee most always referred to them as my boys. They grew up to be handsome, strong, and sturdy young men. Although they were grown now they showed no interest in leaving the comfortable Ruark nest. They really saw no need since they had almost everything they needed at home. Their mother was a great cook and Carey helped her with the wash and keeping their clothes mended. She even shined their shoes for the Friday night dances in Salisbury. If the truth was known their mother and sister would have been much happier and a lot less tired if Lee's boys did leave home.

One time when Carey was very young she heard someone ask Lee how many children he had. He replied very proudly, "Well so far I have three magnificent sons and one daughter!" Needless to say, this made her very sad and she never forgot it.

Lee encouraged his boys to stay and help him on the farm. His big ambition was to own the largest sawmill in the county and his boys were a large part of his dream. He also planned to be the biggest land owner around and with his profits from his hard work he hoped to build Sarah the finest home in the area. It would be so fine most of the people in town would ride by just to gawk at it.

True, Lee's boys did help their father on the farm a bit. But when the sun went down they were not to be found unless you went into Salisbury and found the noisiest saloon around. If a fight should start you would find the three of them "smack dab in the middle of it!" Just like Lee they loved their whiskey, women, and coon dogs. Sad to say they showed no ambition and no love for the land or their father's God.

Whenever his boys didn't come home after the dances in Salisbury Lee's normal routine was to rise early in the morning before Sarah was up and drive his buckboard into town. There he would do his duty as the father of his three rambunctious boys and get them all out of jail. He and the sheriff had a special plan to make the bail for his boys. When the constable rode into town once a year there was no record of any Ruarks ever being arrested.

Lee was always greeted cordially by the sheriff and his deputy. After pleasantries were exchanged Lee would take two bottles filled to the cork with what Sarah called, "The Devil's Brew" from his saddle bag. He would place them carefully on the sheriff's desk. Then he would lift the cell keys from the peg on the wall and unlock the cell which held his boys. They would file out silently and climb quietly onto Lee's buckboard.

It was always a long silent ride home. When they pulled into the yard Lee spoke sternly, "Not a word of this to your Meh! Do you understand?"

With their heads hanging down low and their eyes averted three subdued young men spoke all together, "Yes, sir!"

Lee was positive Sarah didn't know any part of this. Later on when I was older she told me, "I sure loved my old fool. He thought he had pulled the wool over my eyes. I just let him think I was stupid. But I got a good lesson watching old Mr. Owl sitting in a tree. The more he heard the less he spoke. And the less he spoke the more he learned. He was a real wise old bird!"

(So early in my life I learned to stay very quiet and keep my eyes and ears open like Mr. Owl. And I did learn a lot!)

I'm not sure if it was true or not but some people around town started a rumor about Lee and the sheriff. They claimed the sheriff became the town drunk in his old age. Most everyone was quick to lay the blame for his downfall on Lee. They said the sheriff's drinking problem was caused by Lee's boys getting arrested nearly every weekend and Lee being so quick to "pay" their bail.

Chapter 8 – Birth of Afrey

It was a still and silent night. There was not a sound in the room except for the silent prayer from Sarah, *"Please God let him live."* The doctor held up the scrawny new baby and gave him a sharp hard slap on his small bottom. The latest addition to the Ruark family gave a little yelp and began to whimper softly. *"Thank you, Jesus!"* Sarah sighed as the midwife handed Afrey to her. She held her tiny newborn close to her bosom and tried to encourage him to suckle. The old doctor looked at Lee who had stood helplessly by and said, "Son, you have just seen a real miracle here tonight."

The midwife had never seen a baby born so little and she quickly spread the news of Afrey's birth. When their neighbors came to see the new baby Sarah heard the whispered comments they made between themselves: "My goodness, he's such a little bitty thing." "It wasn't a good sign." "He never struggled or cried as he was being born." "He just seemed to drift into this life." "It just wasn't natural!"

True Afrey was quiet and small and he never grew real big and he was never rough and rowdy like the other three Ruark boys. He was certainly not a hell raiser and no one ever heard a cuss word or a word of complaint from him. He had lovely blond hair and skin so white. It was much like the color of Sarah's company china. His blue eyes were the color of the morning sky. His cheerful smile always covered the fact he had to tolerate almost constant pain. He was the peacemaker in the Ruark family. When he was only eight years old he knew exactly what to say to calm a bad situation when Lee got real upset with his other three boys. Although Sarah tried hard not to show any partiality toward any of her children Afrey became the child closest to her heart. She knew his pain and suffered it with him. She spent many lonely nights softly singing her favorite hymns while rocking him gently to sleep in her creaky old rocking chair.

Chapter 9 – Afrey's Little Mommy

After Afrey's birth, Sarah was left terribly weak. Even though he was very small she was not strong enough to pick him up or carry him around. She had to sit or lie down to let him suckle. She also had to take several short cat naps during the day. The rest of the day she was supposed to sit and rest. The doctor even told her not to sit and rock because she would be using energy she really didn't have. Sarah was not a lazy person. Like Lee she had to keep busy. She did a lot of mending and working on their family quilts. Her youngest daughter, Edna, was sorry to see her mother so worn down. She was also glad in a way because she was given the job of most of Afrey's daily baby care. Toys for children were almost unheard of in those days and Edna had never had a single one. She took charge of Afrey and played with him as though he was a favorite doll baby. She was the first to dress him, taught him his first words, and could not hide her happiness when he took his first steps toward her.

Chapter 10 – Whistling Woman

Eventually, Sarah got better. She had listened to her doctor, rested as he ordered, and she had her strength back. She was so happy after the birth of Afrey her joy could not be contained. She sang her favorite hymns almost endlessly during the day. She had been raised in a house full of brothers. Today she kept remembering a little ditty her oldest brother would whistle when he was very happy. Her mother used to say a lady never whistled and she never had, at least when anyone was near. One of her brothers taught her how to whistle when they were way out in the woods where no one could hear them. She had been a good student, practiced a lot, and really enjoyed whistling.

Now on this particular day she was a grownup lady in the yard hanging her family's clothes on the line to dry. She had no idea anybody was anywhere around. She puckered up her lips and whistled her brother's favorite little ditty just as loudly as she could. She even did a couple of little hopping and skipping dance steps to go with the tune. Lee coughed his usual warning and came around the corner of the house. Sarah didn't know if he was angry or had he been amused? He just stood and stared for a minute and then mumbled, "A whistlin' woman or a crowin' hen ain't fit company for God or man."

Chapter 11 – Ruark Education

Those days very few girls got to go to school. Sarah's education had been just old fashioned home schooling. She had been taught at home by her mother. She learned how to cook, wash clothes, and do house work in general. Her mother stressed a good wife always listened to her husband and never questioned his authority. Her grandmother explained if Sarah did these things it would not matter so much who her father was. Her husband would not mind she had nothing to give him except her wedding quilt when she came into his home.

Lee was the oldest child in his family. When he was in the fourth grade his father died of consumption. With no man in the family he had to drop out of school, take care of his younger brother and help his mother on their farm. He was fortunate enough to get a part time job with a man who taught him how to walk through a stand of timber and estimate to the penny how much money it would yield after being cut. He would often brag a bit saying, "Maybe I didn't get a proper education. I just went to the school of hard knocks! And I've learned a whole lot they don't teach in a real school!"

But he and Sarah both valued an education. They wanted all of their children to complete school at least to the fifth grade. This was probably because they neither one had the opportunity to get the schooling they wanted.

Their daughter, Carey, convinced her mother and father she would not need a certificate from school. A marriage license was the only certificate she wanted. She was a real homebody and looking forward to being married and having a home of her own just like her mother.

Lee's three older boys, Elmer, Johnny, and Roy, had no interest in sitting in a boring school room when they could be fishing, hunting, or gambling. They dug in their heels and stood their ground. Lee excused their being so stubborn by saying, "Sarah you know 'you can lead a horse to water but you sure can't make them drink!' Besides they are a bit too big for me to persuade them with a belt in my old wood shed."

Sarah silently thought, *"Lee Bahnum you never did give those boys the whippings they so much needed. I've peeked in the window of your old wood shed more than once and seen you thumping an old bag of chicken feed with your belt while those marvelous sons of yours were screaming and yelping like you were killing them. Maybe if you gave them a few real whippings they might not have turned out so lazy and reckless."* As usual Sarah had just kept silent. To be honest Lee's boys weren't totally bad. They did help Lee a little more on the farm as he grew older. Edna stayed in school until she got her fifth grade certificate. She really should have finished school and become a teacher. She even helped her mother, Sarah, learn how to read a little bit and print some of the words she needed for the stories she loved to tell.

Edna too had dreams like Sarah and Lee. She shared the same dream her mother had. She wanted to write books for children and get them published and sold everywhere. Like her father, she believed she could make a lot of money and she would be able to buy a beautiful house for her mother to live in some day.

Sarah and Lee both wanted Afrey to go to school when he reached his fifth birthday. But he was not strong enough to walk the two miles to school with Edna and he had to remain home.

Chapter 12 – Afrey's Teacher

Though he was too weak to walk to school Afrey eagerly waited at the end of their lane for his big sister, Edna, to return home each day. She then became the teacher and he would be the student. She took the time and really enjoyed teaching him what she had learned in school every day.

Afrey learned his letters and how to read. He enjoyed working with numbers and was very good at arithmetic. He had a poor weak body but a very keen mind. He was a quick learner and was soon reading anything he could get his hands on. Edna's teacher, Miss Courtney, sent home many first rate books he could enjoy and read with ease. To his amazement she also sent him three books about violins. They helped him understand about their strings and notes. One of the books she gave him was full of popular songs of the year and how to play them.

Chapter 13 – Self-Taught Musician

Afrey taught himself to play Lee's fiddle using the music books sent home by Edna's teacher, Miss Courtney. He watched his father playing too. He also loved to entertain the family by imitating his father's fiddle playing, complete with all of the whooping and feet stomping to the beat of Lee's rowdy old dance tunes.

During Afrey's performances Carey held her sides and giggled like a school girl. Edna danced around the floor laughing hysterically. Lee's three older boys had a good old time laughing loudly, stomping their feet, clapping their hands to the music, and giving out a lusty "Yee Ha" when it was needed. Sarah proudly watched her angel boy and listened intently to every note.

When she heard Lee's loud cough as he came around the corner of the barn and started up the long path leading to the house Sarah quickly sounded the alarm, "Your father's coming!" Everyone scurried around and quickly found something to do so they would all appear to be industrious. Afrey would switch into one of his mother's favorite hymns. Sarah would pick up her sewing basket. Carey grabbed a ladle and began stirring the contents of their big kettle of food hanging in the fireplace. Edna began setting their plates on the table for supper. The three oldest boys quickly grabbed their pocketknives and began to whittle busily.

Lee never let them know he sneaked up to the porch, peeked in the window, and watched their antics. He'd laugh to himself, *"I'm not as dumb as I look. They are just having good clean fun."*

He would sneak back down to the yard and make a commotion stepping up onto the porch. He'd also give another warning cough to let them know he was coming in. He never made any comment about Afrey using his fiddle. He simply gave him a long look and a quiet sigh. He'd reach for his fiddle and hang it on the wall peg near the fireplace. Then he'd give Afrey a small smile and a quick wink. Afrey secretly smiled back and gave Lee a small wink. Then he thought to himself, *"I know my father ain't mad with me. And I know he's really proud of me too!"*

Chapter 14 – Lee's Plans for Afrey

With his boys helping a bit on the farm Lee had a little more free time to think some things out. He was not a big talker but he did a lot of thinking when he got the opportunity. Though he never bragged out loud about Afrey, Lee was really very proud of what his little man had accomplished.

One day when he was out working in his fields Lee's thoughts started racing through his head. *"Being able to read anything he wants, understanding 'rithmetic, and even learning to play my fiddle all by his self. Now, that's really something! He's a lot like me except for being so body weak. I ain't ever had any real schooling. The only schooling I ever got was from the school of hard knocks. But I could always learn anything I put my mind to. Afrey's mind works like mine just like quicksilver. I only have to show or tell him something once and he's got it for ever. He's so frail he'll most likely never be able to do a real man's job. If I could swing it and get myself my own sawmill he might be able to take care of those jobs like keeping records, bills, and receipts. I hate to admit it but that's something I really don't like to do. He'd be perfect for keeping my books!"*

He continued to think, *"He's not one to waste his time chasing women, dancing, or gambling. He'd make an excellent business partner for me! I'd best talk my plan over with Sarah right now before I forget it!"*

Chapter 15 – A Death and a Funeral

Lee simply refused to believe Afrey was not to be much longer in this world.

Sarah and Edna had seen the signs though. Afrey was getting tired a lot quicker now. He wasn't eating much and he had a lot more shortness of breath. He was getting weaker and his cough was much worse. They did their best to make him stronger and keep him alive and well. But he caught a bad case of pneumonia in the winter of 1906 when he was only ten years old. He drifted out of this world as quietly and peacefully as he had entered it.

Afrey had a small private funeral. Sarah and Lee picked out a little plot of land for him in a grove of trees on a small hill overlooking their farm. A preacher came out from town and spoke a brief service for him. Sarah said a short prayer through her tears. She thanked God for sending Afrey to their family. He had brought laughter and joy into all of their lives. She ended her prayer saying, "Darling boy, we will see you on the other side in Heaven's city of gold where there will be no more sorrow or pain."

Each of Lee's three boys said a few words about Afrey and how he would be missed. Everyone was surprised to see Lee brush away a tear, quickly tune his fiddle, and play the same hymn Sarah sang so many times to her beautiful boy. Sarah, Carey, and Edna wept softly. The mourning family trudged solemnly back to the house. Afrey was gone. But he was kept in their hearts and never forgotten.

Chapter 16 - Fred's Birth

With a loud bellering cry Frederick entered the Ruark family two years later. The neighbors claimed he could be heard for miles. They came to see the newborn. Little Fred entertained his guests by yelling and screaming at the top of his lungs in a very demanding way. The visitors laughed and remarked: "He will be a determined young man!" "He ought to be able to make himself heard." "Wow! He is sure full of piss and vinegar!" "You might have a hard time training this little mustang!" "You're going to have your hands full with this one, Lee!"

After each comment Lee strutted around like an ole proud peacock and grinned from ear to ear. Sarah thought to herself, *"He's strutting like a peacock and grinning just like an old possum!"*

Sarah had said she wanted this new baby to hold to her bosom. She knew he would never fill the void she felt when Afrey died. But she was much stronger and thought the extra work she would need to care for this new one would help ease the pain she still felt. She was already beginning to wonder if this had really been a good idea. She just went around the room quietly serving cake and cider to her guests. She continued to think, *"Yes, Lee will get all the credit if Fred turns out good and I'll get all the blame if he turns out bad."*

Of course she never voiced these thoughts out loud. She seldom spoke out against Lee during their marriage especially in front of his friends. She just stuffed all of her emotions deep down inside again and never vented them. At times it felt like someone was choking her when she wanted to burst open and say what she really felt or believed. Her mother had told her many times if she wanted a happy marriage she must always remain a silent obedient wife and bow to the authority of her husband. Sarah could not forget about the many times she had heard her father and mother having bitter arguments. God knew how much she wanted a happy marriage! She had always bowed to the authority of Lee. She had stayed quiet so much and for so long she often thought she would surely die if she did not speak up. But like a good obedient wife Sarah remained silent.

Chapter 17 – Courting Days

A nice young man, Tom Mumford Junior, had showed an interest in Carey. Because he was much like her father Lee was completely pleased with Tom and quickly gave his permission for their courting. Tom and Carey often took long rides in his fancy surrey along the banks of the Wicomico River. And they enjoyed many picnics in Lee's woods. After Lee thought about how he had courted Sarah he gave Tom a no nonsense warning about proper courting behaviors. "Now Tom I don't want you acting like an animal with my Carey. I just want you to respect her. Keep your head on your shoulders and your hands in your pockets. Don't do any thing stupid because if you do you will regret the day you were born and sure as hell you will have to pay this fiddler!" Tom clearly understood Lee would hunt him down and beat him half to death if he acted improper toward Carey.

Sarah was having a similar talk with Carey. She was reminding her daughter it was a woman's job to start out right by controlling her man without letting him know she was in charge. "Just remember a man will only go as far as you let him!" Neither Tom nor Carey was totally sure of what Lee's and Sarah's warnings were all about. But they had a general idea. They had been raised on a farm. Tom behaved like a perfect gentleman and Carey was a real proper lady.

Chapter 18 – Marriage Concerns

Lee was very pleased with the idea of Carey marrying Tom. He silently thought. *"It could work out mighty good! If Carey marries young Tom it would be most advantageous because his father's farm joins up to my land. Mr. Mumford is real old. He only has one son. When old Mr. Mumford dies his farm will likely be passed to young Tom and my Carey. Then if anything happens to young Tom his property would go to my Carey!"*

Sarah was a bit more reluctant about Tom. She liked him but she was also aware he had both the good and the bad traits her husband Lee showed from time to time. This troubled her a great deal. She was sure Carey, a strong willed outspoken woman, would never be able to hold her tongue as she had done so often with Lee. She believed too they would have many loud disagreeable times. Sarah thought to herself, *"People are getting married and divorced too easy these days. They don't believe in pulling together to make their marriage work and making it last! It's got so you hear too much about going back to your mother. Well my baby raising days are over. If Carey and Tom ever part I sure don't look forward to Carey bringing home a bunch of younguns for me to raise up in my old age!"*

Because of these fears Sarah cautioned her daughter and tried to persuade her to wait until some finer young man came along. Carey was afraid if she refused Tom she might become a lonely old maid like Miss Hailey who lived all by herself down the road. "After all," Carey argued, "Most all my friends are already married and Sadie even has a little one hanging around her skirts." Carey stressed the fact Tom loved her. "He doesn't have to marry me! He wants to marry me! He doesn't mind I'm so plain looking and I have no dowry except my wedding quilt to take to my husband's house!"

Carey ended her pleading by wailing, "Oh why can't you understand? I'm almost nineteen now and I love Tom the same as you love my father with his faults and all!"

After hearing Carey's reasons for wanting to marry young Tom Sarah was still a bit reluctant but gave her blessing and agreed to Carey and Tom getting married.

Chapter 19 - Dish-Cuss-Shuns

Sarah did not hear much of what the preacher was saying at Carey and Tom's wedding ceremony. She was lost deep in her own thoughts. She recalled both the good and the bad memories she and Lee had shared over the years. A little smile touched her lips as she remembered back to the many discussions she and Lee had during the first years of their marriage.

Lee did most of the arguing. Sarah most always kept her mouth shut and just pretended to listen to him. But when he pushed her last button and she had enough she would grab a plate and throw it at his head. She always missed. But it made him so mad he'd grab another one and slam it onto the floor. Each thrown dish was accompanied by a verbal reminder of some previous hurt or fault not forgotten or forgiven. They tossed their prized dishes back and forth. When they got down to just a few pieces left Lee would usually burst out laughing and Sarah would join him. Lee would then likely say, "Mulie, you sure are a mighty stubborn woman. I guess that's one of the reasons that made me want to marry you. Our life will never be boring. We'll most likely run out of dishes to eat on though."

Then he'd chase her around the kitchen and give her a great big hug and attempt to kiss her. She'd brush him off laughing and say, "Lee, quit your fooling around! The children are watching!" They were too! They were hiding in their beds under their quilts pretending to be asleep. It was great fun to watch their parents argue. It was just like a show. They always giggled and clapped their hands when the discussions ended with Lee giving Sarah a great long kiss. Lee and Sarah would both be laughing and her face would get just as red as those berries on the cherry tree out in the yard beside the old outhouse.

Early the next morning Lee would ride in town to the Salisbury General Store to buy some new dishes. The store clerk would just smile knowingly and say, "Guess you and

Sarah must have had another serious dish cuss shun!" Then they would both have a good laugh.

In spite of their dish cuss shuns, as they came to be called, Sarah and Lee both dearly loved one another in their own way until the day they died.

Chapter 20 – Pig in a Poke

Sarah came out of her trip down memory lane just as the preacher said, "Carey and Tom, I now pronounce you man and wife."

The ceremony was over and there were tears of happiness in Sarah's eyes. Lee handed her his handkerchief and laughed out loudly saying, "I never could understand why women always cry at weddings!"

He shook hands with Tom and said, "Well it is official now! Welcome to the Ruark family. You've changed Carey's name to Mumford. Just remember though she'll always be a Ruark and from now on you'll be my son. Remember too you took my Carey just like a 'pig in a poke'. You can't ever return her. There was no guarantee from me or my wife! "

The bride and groom and all their wedding guests joined in with Lee and Sarah and had a hearty laugh. Sarah just hugged the newlyweds and whispered, "My prayer for you is for your married life to be as happy as Lee's and mine has been! Remember too, being married takes hard work from both of you."

Someone asked Lee about his marriage to Sarah. With a big wink and his eyes just sparkling he answered, "Well, it's been a lot more good than bad!"

Chapter 21 - Free at Last

Carey had moved into her new husband's home and was quite content. Truthfully she felt free at last. She was the mistress of her own home. She did not miss Elmer, Johnny, or Roy at all. They were still living with her parents. This was probably one of the reasons she was so quick to accept Tom's attention and want to get married. Cooking, washing, and cleaning up after her three, not so magnificent, brothers probably played a large part in her so quickly accepting Tom's proposal.

Baby Fred was now an active little toddler trying out everyone's patience. Elmer had grown into the town hell raiser. He liked his women and his whiskey. Johnny was trying to follow in his foot steps. He also thought a good fight was the most exciting part of being a man. Whenever Roy was allowed to go with his brothers and his father he usually came home bragging about how he had twirled and whirled the prettiest girl at the dance. Unlike his father he left many of his ladies with broken promises and broken hearts. Lee no longer bailed his boys out of their situations. He said they were grown and now it was up to them to make their own choices in life, good or bad, and take the consequences. Still none of Lee's boys seemed to be thinking about moving away from home any time soon.

Carey did miss Edna though. They had good times together and had become very close. Before Carey went to Tom's house to live she taught Edna how to 'shake a broom' at her brothers to get them out of the house and help her father more because he was getting older.

Carey also taught Edna how to keep a house neat as a pin, be a good cook, show a cheerful disposition, and all the other desired traits of a perfect housewife. She believed those things would prove to be mighty useful when some young man bought her little sister's basket at one of the church socials.

Chapter 22 – The Tale Teller

Now Carey was gone Edna drew closer to her mother and tagged after her so much Sarah often tripped over her and they would both fall down together. When this happened they would just sit there on the floor and laugh loudly. Sarah would tell Edna one of her favorite little stories. Sarah's memory was filled with those stories which she had learned in her home. She had heard them from her grandfather who was called Wiseman. He gave Sarah the name of Tale Teller because she remembered all the stories and could tell them almost as well as he did.

Sarah loved telling her tales about tiny little animals like mice, rabbits, owls, and other small creatures who could talk, reason, and figure out how to solve their difficult dilemmas. These stories also taught little children the importance of making the right choices to solve some of their problems in life. Sarah's stories were often full of sadness but they always had a happy ending because wise choices had been made.

Edna loved hearing all of her mother's stories. Years later when she was grown and married to Robert Pottle she told them to her own children, Robert, Nina, and Norman. They enjoyed her stories as much as she had when she was a young girl listening to her mother.

In later years Edna's daughter, Nina, showed the same talents as her mother and her grandmother, Sarah. She was a very gifted storyteller and also drew pictures for the stories she wrote. But like her mother and grandmother Nina was kept too busy with her own children, Bobby and Jo Anne. She had no time to pursue her dream and never learned how to get her books published.

Despite her heavy work load during the day Sarah had always felt guilty stealing the hours late at night for herself. She claimed these precious hours as 'My Time.' Carey was content in her new home with her husband, Tom. In the Ruark home when supper was done Fred would soon be sound asleep in his little loft room. After she cleared up the dishes Edna usually went to bed early too. Lee, Elmer, and Johnny, went to town "just for a short spell." Roy was finally allowed to tag along with them. He had promised not to brag about all of his beautiful women he had twirled around. Sarah knew the men would not come in until early morning. She continued to think about becoming a famous writer some day. However she still had problems writing her stories down on paper. Only her brothers had been allowed to go to school. Of course they never saw the need to teach their sister what they had learned. Sarah was afraid as she grew older she would forget a lot of the stories she had kept in her mind. She used a lot of her 'My Time' to draw pictures to help her remember her stories. She hoped she would be able to pass them on to her grandbabies some day.

Chapter 23 - Lee's Little Shadow

Lee's three oldest boys were grown or so they believed. They had finally moved out. They were staying on the other side of Salisbury now and had taken a job with old Mr. Baxter. Lee was a bit concerned about the kind of work they did for him. It was strongly suspected Mr. Baxter had a well-hidden whiskey still and had recruited Lee's boys to deliver his rot gut. Lee reasoned to himself *"Well, they made their choice for good or bad and they are all grown up. If they get caught delivering Baxter's booze it's out of my hands."* Lee had no boys at home to bail out of jail now!

Sarah reminded Lee his young son Fred was still at home and he was growing into a very unpredictable child. One minute he was a loving helpful son. But the next minute he was like a different person. His father seemed to enjoy encouraging him in his little escapades. Both Lee and Fred had the same sparkling twinkle in their eyes and the same mischievous grin. Of course Lee said he didn't see any real harm in Fred's behaviors. He often said with pride, "He's the spitting image of me when I was a lot younger!"

Once he called his youngest son "the tricker" and this name really stuck through Fred's whole life. He got a lot of pleasure out of pulling what he thought was a good joke on anyone. He never actually told a lie. But he had a reputation for bending the truth just a little to get a good laugh like his father. Sarah once made an excuse for their behavior by saying, "Well I'm not sure which one is the worst. They're just like two peas in a pod."

Fred was really glad his older brothers had gone to work for Mr. Baxter. Many times in the past when Lee had thought his boys were out working in his fields they would often hide, slip into town, and head for the nearest saloon. Then Lee would make Fred go find them. Fred had to ride Lee's sulky ole mule

Sully. She was so stubborn his brothers would get home before he found them. Then he'd be the one his father would scold.

Fred's brothers were always trying to get him in trouble with his father. He didn't like it when they called him names like runt or pest and sometimes worse when Lee wasn't around. He didn't like it when they chased him away from his father either.

Sarah loved her youngest son but Lee was the parent who was responsible for spoiling Fred rotten when he was a baby. Now he was older Lee still seemed to enjoy Fred's little pranks. He was really kind of proud of his boy's spunkiness. Fred was really good about sneaking around corners and hearing things he wasn't supposed to hear. He often heard his father laugh and brag to the other men in Salisbury about some funny thing his boy had done. Sarah failed to enjoy the many tricks Fred played on others. She could not understand him at all. Some of his pranks were down right hurtful.

Fred's plan was to become his father's little man. He felt very secure of his position as Lee's favorite. He began to strut around in his father's footsteps like a proud little rooster. If Lee stopped too suddenly and turned around he would nearly fall over Fred. "Oh. Oh!" Lee would exclaim, "There's my little shadow!" Then they would have a good laugh together.

Lately Sarah was not finding Fred's antics very amusing. What was funny when he was a baby was no longer cute. She worried about him and prayed daily for him to change his ways. She believed if he danced to the tune he would have to pay the fiddler some day. In other words his mean tricks would catch up with him.

Chapter 24 – Sarah Gives Up

Sarah believed in signs. She thought Fred's behavior and his father's lack of proper discipline was a sure sign she should not struggle with her son's behavior any more. "Lee, you know our Good Book says if you spare the rod you'll spoil the child." She spoke her other thoughts silently. *"I should just let Fred make his own choices and be what ever he will be. I love him as much as I love my own life. I must face it though. He's just a natural born schemer and a schemer he will always be. I guess he doesn't mean to do any real harm. He just doesn't think ahead and he can't see the end of his tricks. He believes they are only fun."*

After much thinking about Fred during the night Sarah prayed silently, *"Father I am just bone tired and so weak. Forgive me but I can't deal with this anymore. I truly love my son but I am going to have to give Fred back to you! Do as you please with him. The only thing I ask and pray is that you will save his soul before he is too old to change."* Sarah fell asleep sobbing softly.

Chapter 25 – Another Bundle

Lee had gone out early to tend to his animals. Sarah woke with a sick throbbing headache. The room seemed to be spinning around just like the merry-go-round at the county fair last year. She knew it really couldn't be. But she lay in her bed and held tightly onto the bed posts anyway. After a few minutes the spinning stopped. She was so nauseous she did not make it to the night time chamber pot. She threw up right in the center of the bed. There she sat in the middle of it and thought about this sickness she had been feeling in the mornings lately. Now she realized what was causing it. She knew this was a sure sign a little bundle from Heaven would be arriving soon.

"Forgive me Lord," she prayed silently. *"I thought I was all done with this baby birthing thing. I know this little bundle will be a gift from Heaven. But I am only human and right now I can only think about the bundle of baby clothes I'll have to wash on my old scrub board. After giving up on Fred and turning him over to you I'm really surprised you'd trust me with another little one. Lord, truly I am thrilled! I ask you only, please let this one be a girl and please please give her great health, strong ambition, and determination. Thank you, Jesus. Amen!"*

Chapter 26 – Lee's New Love

When young Fred heard his parents having a loud discussion about a new baby coming into their home he wasn't too concerned. In spite of all his pranks he still felt very sure of himself. He soon realized though his position as Lee's favorite child was not going to last much longer.

Emma was born on February 14, 1910 and everything in the world seemed to change. Sarah said, "Lee Bahnum fell in love again. He didn't make much fuss over Carey and Edna when they were born because they were just girls and I'd be more in charge of them. When Emma was born Lee leaned down to look her over. She grabbed his big finger with her tiny hand and would not let it go." Later in life Sarah said, "Emma just got a hold of Lee's heart strings at the same time!"

For the life of him Fred could not understand how anyone could ooh and ah over her? He wondered to himself, *"How could anyone love a fat thing like Emma? She is so fat she looks like she has no chin. Her hair is dark black and she's got enough for three babies. She howls all the time day and night. She sounds just like the old stray cat I threw off of the barn roof two or three times to see if it could really fly like Brian Hoppes told me."*

(It never did fly!)

Chapter 27 - Cry Baby Cry

Fred's favorite pastime now was to find some new way to tease Emma and make her cry. When she was only a year old she loved sucking on her rag tit which Sarah had made with a small square of material from her sewing basket. There was a glob of molasses in the center of the cloth and it was tied up by the four corners. It was almost like magic the way this old rag would keep her quiet. Fred was now three years old and every chance he got he would take it from her and throw it across the floor. He seemed to get a lot of pleasure by making her yowl. For some unknown reason he really enjoyed his power to make her cry.

Sarah never caught Fred in his meanness and she was amazed her baby girl could spit her molasses tit out so far from her cradle. Sarah told Lee about it in a joking way, "She might just be a girl but she'll most likely out spit you when she's grown!" With his usual Irish twinkle in his eyes Lee would smile at Sarah and then wink slyly at Fred. He wasn't really much of a talker. But he knew a lot more than he let on. He knew exactly how Emma's molasses tit got so far across the room!

Chapter 28 – Wait and See

Fred still enjoyed making his little sister cry a lot. Sarah had given up. She made no attempt to change his behaviors. Lee knew what was going on when he heard Emma crying. He seldom interfered because he figured Fred's teasing would make her stronger for hard times and disappointments when she was older. One day though when he saw Fred teasing her he said very softly, "You know Fred she's just a little one now. But she's got a good memory. When she gets a little bigger she might even be able to whip you arm wrestling! I don't take my beauty for being a weak little namby pamby. You might get your laughs from making her cry now while she's just a little one. I'll bet you won't be able to devil her and make her cry when she gets bigger. And I'll make you another bet too. The man ain't been born who will be able to make her cry when she's grown up!"

Fred came back with "Aw, she's just a girl! You're always favoring her. She won't be able to do much of anything except maybe keep some man's house clean and put his meals on the table.

Lee laughed, "Wait and see, Fred! Just wait and see!"

Chapter 29 – School Shenanigans

Fred was five years old and in the first grade when some of the older boys got him to put a tack on his teacher's chair. The new teacher, Miss Rachel, got the point! But she didn't squeal out. She reached under her bottom and gingerly removed the tack. She didn't want to give the guilty one any attention. The whole class erupted in a laughing fit. She noticed all the boys were clapping Fred on the back at recess and every one of them was still giggling. She knew who the culprit was. She had his number and the first of many notes went home for his inappropriate school behaviors. Sarah was always the one to put on her hat and go to have a talk with Fred's teacher.

Time passed quickly and Fred filled this time with numerous other tricks. His behaviors brought many more notes from his frustrated teacher to his deeply worried mother.

Fred became the ring leader of his school buddies because he could always find unique ways to bedevil Miss Rachel. He and the other boys had a great time playing tricks on his long suffering teacher. She had scheduled many talks with his mother to discuss his behaviors in class during his first year of school. After getting a full report Sarah had tried everything she knew to change Fred's behavior. She used bribes, early bed times, and even tried withholding his favorite desserts. She also tried giving him a little of her egg money to spend in town if he could go a week without stepping over the line at school. But he did not show any improvement. Sarah finally told Lee she was going to give up trying to change Fred. She just couldn't cope with his bad behaviors any more. Lee thought, *"She's just making a mountain out of a mole hill."*

The notes kept coming! This time Sarah had really not been feeling very well. She tried to persuade Lee as the head of the family to attend the talks requested by Miss Rachel.

Sarah told Lee she had not been able to change any of Fred's bad behavior and she suggested he might have more success in straightening his youngest son out. She continued with, "What he really needs is a man to train him up in the way he should go and when he is old he will not depart from it just like it says in our bible. We both know it also says, 'If you spare the rod you'll spoil the child.' She ended with, "I really believe you are the one to straighten him out and get him on the right path. He shows a lot more respect for you than he does for me. He will do most anything you ask him to do." Lee swallowed her flattering words. He again took her bait, hook, line, and sinker. He agreed to go to the school and have a talk with Miss Rachel. Grabbing his hat he raced out of the door. But he was mumbling loudly all the way out to the barn about two women not being able to handle a boy just five years old!

Chapter 30 - A Lasting Impression

Fred was now six and all the boys in his second grade class enjoyed being a part of all his tricks. It was just too much for Sarah to handle and she had asked Miss Rachel to please address all school letters to her husband, Lee. But Lee was now getting a bit tired of all those notes sent to him. They were starting to interfere with his scheduled work. This visit to school was, as usual, concerning Fred's smart mouth and another outlandish prank. Miss Rachel told Lee Fred's latest escapade was to fill the wood stove, used for heating the school room, with a lot of dried cow chips. Then he waited for her to start a nice roaring fire. The smell was unbearable and she had to dismiss school early. The reward for Fred's behavior was a day off from school. He and all the other boys ran laughing to the nearest swimming hole. It was too cold to go swimming but they could sit around and brag about all the wicked things they had got away with in the past years. They even tried smoking some monkey cigars which grew on those trees along the banks of the creek. It was a great day for all of them. It was especially good for Fred. The boys had bragged on how clever he was. Fred had really become the leader of the pack! He felt like a real hero and swelled up with pride just like an old horn toad.

Miss Rachel began with telling Lee since Fred was now six years old and in the second grade he was old enough to be setting a good example for the other first graders. She ended her report by saying Fred really needed a punishment from his father which would leave a lasting impression.

Lee listened intently to the teacher until she finished with her talking. He agreed with her a strong punishment was needed in this case and certainly would be given for Fred's latest behavior.

Then he gave Fred a severe warning look. "You just wait till we get home young man! You are six years old and you are still acting like a little baby boy! It's past time for you to hitch up your britches and learn something in school! You sure are going to get what you've been asking for!" Miss Rachel smiled and nodded her head in approval. She felt badly Sarah had not been able to make any changes in Fred's behavior. She was sure this time he would learn a long over-due lesson from his father. "Thank you! Mr. Ruark. Thank you!" She smiled broadly as she pictured Fred in the family woodshed with his father using his belt to make a deep and lasting impression on Fred's little rear end!

Neither Lee nor Fred spoke the whole way home. Funny though the ride home in his father's buckboard should have seemed a lot shorter then it did walking. But it didn't! It seemed a lot longer than the two miles he had to walk to and from school in the rain or snow. This ride with his mad silent father seemed the longest ride Fred ever had. He feared the worst whipping in the world. He was very relieved when they got home and Lee just rushed to the barn and began brushing Major down. As Fred took off to run and play he silently promised himself never to try his funny cow chip prank again. And he never did!

Chapter 31 – Getting Even

Emma was now four and she was able to run anywhere she wanted. Fred was six and had the job of watching out for her. He was to make sure she didn't get lost or hurt. Now it was her turn to get even with Fred for some of the tricks he played on her when she was just a baby. Her favorite thing was to hide from him and he had an awful time finding her. This got him in trouble with his parents when he was supposed to bring her into the house. Fred didn't think he should be responsible for her. He complained to his father, "Just because she's your favorite she gets away with a lot! She's always hiding and getting me in trouble when I can't find her!" Lee just smiled and said, "I told you she would get even with you some day for all the times you teased her when she was a little baby. And I told you too you should have treated her nicer. Now it's her turn to get even with you!"

The next time Fred called Emma to come in for her lunch she hid from him and wouldn't come. He got mad and when he found her he gave her a real hard spanking! She didn't cry but she got very angry. She waited patiently and later on she caught him taking a nap out in the yard. She picked up a large heavy tree branch, took a running leap, and hit him on his head with it. Knocked him out cold!

Then she walked calmly into the house. "Well, baby girl, where's your big brother?" Lee asked.

Emma answered sweetly, "I think he's sleeping under the apple tree. I tried to wake him to come in and eat but he wouldn't get up." Lee went to the door and hollered loudly for Fred.

There was no answer. "Tarnation, why doesn't that boy answer me? I'll have to go get him and give him a good switching too."

Lee found Fred unconscious and brought him quickly to

the pump bench. He pumped some really cold water on Fred's head. When Fred came around Lee asked him what happened. Not wanting his father to know Emma had knocked him out, Fred said, "I ran and bumped into our old apple tree."

Lee asked, "Did you see him, Emma?"

"Nope," she replied calmly, "I found a big old tree branch and I hit him with it. After I hit him for spanking me I tried to wake him up but he just laid there. So I came on in to eat lunch."

Much to Fred's embarrassment his father had a good laugh. "When I was just a very young boy in my home country, Ireland, I had an aunt. Your baby sister is a lot like she was. Her name was Janey and we used to call her Lady Janey because she was so tough and bossy. Like your baby sister she was also a very determined young lady. She had a hot temper and a small amount of patience. But she could always wait for the right time to pay you back. Yep, Emma just doesn't suit your baby sister for her name. From now on we're going to call her Lady Janey!"

Fred mumbled, "Well I'm not calling her Lady Janey! We could just call her Janey."

"That's fair enough!" Lee laughed, "Now it's all settled! Janey, it'll be!"

Smiling at Emma, Lee laughed again, "Come on Janey, let's all have our lunch before your mother puts it away and gives it to us for our supper!

Chapter 32 – The Final Straw

Fear of getting a real whipping from his father had encouraged Fred to stay out of trouble for what felt like forever to him. Now he was seven years old and in the third grade when he tried a new trick in school. Once again a note from Miss Rachel arrived at the Ruark home. It was time to have another meeting and discuss Fred's latest inappropriate school behavior. Lee put on his hat, hitched Major to his buckboard, and went to have another talk with Miss Rachel. As usual Fred's teacher did most of the talking and Lee did most of the listening. She told him this time Fred had talked some of the other boys into teasing one of her best and brightest students. Her voice rose in a very unlady like tone, "I am going to recommend Frederick be removed from any further attendance in this school. I have tried my best but nothing seems to matter to him! This latest trick of his is really like the straw which broke the camel's back! I just can't put up with his misbehaving any more!"

Before Fred's father had a chance to speak, she continued and explained Lou Ann Wilkins, her brightest student, had gone down the path to the outhouse. As she came out Fred and his gang of boys began loudly laughing and chanting.

"Lou Ann, Lou Ann can't even catch a man!
She went to the outhouse to take a shit.
Poor Lou Ann was so broken-hearted
She only farted, farted, farted!"

Miss Rachel came from a very wealthy family and she had been raised to be a proper lady. She was really embaressed to hear Fred and his gang chanting such a horrid rhyme. She was even more embarrassed to repeat their chant to Mr. Ruark. Lee had a very hard time keeping a straight face. He coughed loudly and sounded as though he was choking. But he managed to regain his composure and assured her again Fred would get exactly what was coming to him.

Lee was not able to hide the sparkle in his mischevious eyes and his face was even redder than Miss Rachel's. Her mother had not raised a fool. She could tell Fred's father found this episode very amusing. She knew too Fred would get nothing for it when they got home. "*Well,*" she thought, "*I'm quite sure Fred's behavior will only get worse and more frequent. He will most likely get a pat on the back as praise for his outlandish actions.*"

She covered her displeasure and walked Fred and his father to the schoolhouse door. As she watched them ride down the lane her thoughts were furious! "*That's it! I'm finished with this whole teaching business! I'm just going to apply for a secretary job at the new electric company down town. If these men think their boy's antics are so amusing let's see them try to educate their little hoodlums.*" As she packed up her books and papers for the last time she was smiling broadly.

True to her word, Miss Rachel resigned her teaching position. She said the reason for giving her notice was because it had been too stressful. She was replaced by a young man teacher though because most of the parents believed a man's firm hand would be better suited to make their boys walk the chalk line. After Fred's terrible mean prank poor Lou Ann had broke down crying, ran home, and swore she would never go back to school again. When she heard about the new young man teacher, Mr. Edwards, she returned to school and she ended up marrying him. Well, as Miss Rachel had said Lou Ann was the brightest student in her class.

Chapter 33 - Like Father Like Son

After they had finished their last meeting with Miss Rachel Fred and his father had gone about half a mile from the school in silence. Lee could not hold it any longer. He started to say, "Well Fred I didn't realize we had a poet in our family." But then he broke out laughing as hard as he could. He laughed so loud Fred was afraid he was going to bust a gut or something. Lee ended his laughter with a deep sigh and then he said, "Damn! You sure did play a good one this time!" Then he chuckled some more. Like the many times before when they got home Lee rushed to the barn to brush down Major and as usual there was no belt whipping in the old woodshed for Fred.

This time Fred strutted into the house, tossed a smirking look at his mother, and went quickly up into his loft. After Lee and Sarah had gone to bed Fred heard them arguing about his latest escapade. Lee had seen the humor of Fred's prank and Sarah had not. "Oh hell, Sarah, he's just a boy! Give him some room!" Sarah did not answer. She turned over and pretended to be asleep. Lee continued "Fred is just a high spirited boy. He'll out grow all this foolishness in time." "Yes," Sarah thought, *"Just like your other three magnificent sons Elmer, Johnny, and Roy! It's just a little funny. They've never grown out of their foolishness!"*

Once again she never uttered her thoughts out loud. She just shoved all of her frustration down deep inside of herself like all of the other times. There was no more discussions about Fred's outlandish behaviors.

Lee stayed awake for a while thinking over Fred's latest episode and chuckled silently. He couldn't wait to get to town again and tell his drinking buddies about Fred's latest prank. "*Damn!*" he thought, *"Fred's trick sounds just like something I did when I was his age! I guess the apple don't fall far from the tree."*

Chapter 34 - The Matriarch's Meals

Lee had always encouraged his boys to stay at home after they were grown. He believed someday they would work with him and prosper in a family business venture.

Sarah didn't see this ever happening. She knew Lee's sons didn't have the same ambition as their father. Lee made some of the rules for his family and his farm. Sarah had her own set of do's and don'ts inside the home. I remember once she told me, "I always try not to ruffle Lee's feathers. I just let him think he's the boss. He rules the roost but I rule the rooster!"

One very important rule to both Lee and Sarah came from their bible, "Keep the Sabbath Day holy. It is the Lord's Day. On the seventh day you shall do no work."

It was Thanksgiving and Sarah expected all of her family to come home for her family dinner. All of Lee's outside farm work and all of Sarah's cooking for Sunday was done on Saturday. She arranged everything on her table and covered it with a white linen tablecloth, to keep those pesky flies off of the food.

Two o'clock was the 'sitting down time.' The Grace would be said by Lee. His "A-Men" was the signal to dig in and the loud talking would begin as well. Edna told me in later years she could actually see the window panes viberate once the Ruarks got started! It seemed like everyone was talking as loud as they could and all at the same time.

The grown-ups always ate first and the children played outside until the grown-ups were finished. Sometimes they would finish eating and push back their chairs. They would continue telling and retelling some interesting story about one of the Ruarks. When their story ended they would often pull their chairs back up to the table and eat some more. The children would still have to wait for them to finish and most of the good food would be all gone! This tradition was carried over for many years.

(When I was a child I used to think, "*Someday I'll be a grown-up and I'll get to eat first before the good food is almost all gone.*" Guess what? When I became a grown up things had changed a lot. Now the children eat first and with full stomachs play happily outside and then we grown ups eat last when the good food is almost all gone!)

The Ruark family all had a great time at those meals. This was their time to share good food and then tell and retell some great stories about something their family had gone through together.

Chapter 35 – Cutting Back Some

It was Thanksgiving time again but Lee's crops had failed pretty badly. This year he and Sarah decided have a Thanksgiving breakfast just for their family. There would be no guests except Lee's three magnificent sons, and Carey with her husband and their baby. Of course Lee's youngest, Edna, Fred, and Janey completed the Ruark family circle.

Sarah was a strict mother and loved all of her children each in a different way. She shared and encouraged each one's dreams and ambitions. She strongly believed her family meals were what held the Ruarks together through good times and bad.

When Sarah rang her dinner bell everyone dashed into the kitchen. The delicious meal she had cooked made the whole house smell just wonderful. She had used her best dishes. There was a red linen tablecloth under her prized crocheted one. She had picked some colorful flowers from her garden and put a small bouquet at each place setting. She had asked Edna to write a short note for each family member to express her pride and love for each of them. Sarah had drawn a small picture on the front of her cards. She placed each card on the plate of the person she had chosen the note for.

Lee said, "Well Sarah you have really outdone yourself with all this delicious smelling chicken and dumplings you made for our Thanksgiving breakfast. And your notes are just as thoughtful and pretty as you are! Now it's time for me to give you an early Christmas present. I'm going to give you a great big kiss right here in front of all our children!"

Sarah started to run but Lee was too quick for her. He caught her and put her over his knee as though to spank her. Everyone was just short of being hysterical with laughter. They all started chanting, "Kiss her! Kiss her! Kiss her!"

He winked and grinned at his family audience of children.

Then he gave her the biggest longest kiss he could to the delight of all! Instead of scolding Lee for his behavior in front of their children, Sarah surprised them all by giving Lee a longer kiss back.

Roy broke the romantic spell by yelling, "O.K., love birds. That's enough now!"

Laughing loudly, Johnny shouted, "Pass me some of your chicken! It sure smells good!"

Chapter 36 – Old Time Christmas

Christmas was here! Lee and Sarah decided to have a practical ole time Christmas since Lee, being a farmer, was still a little short of money. The rooster crowed and the three youngest Ruark children, still at home, were all up. After they woke they each found new shirts folded neatly at the foot of their beds. They looked suspiciously like Sarah had sewn them. There were also some new coveralls just like the ones at the General Store in Salisbury. Brightly shining shoes were setting in neat rows under each of their beds. Knitted woolen hats and mittens were welcome gifts too. They would keep the youngest Ruark children warm and dry on their long walk to and from school. And there on the mantle over the fireplace were three large Christmas stockings Sarah had knitted and filled with sweet candy, a piece of fruit and some walnuts. Edna, Fred, and Janey were all pleased with their gifts and never thought to ask, "Is this all there is?" like many children do today.

Chapter 37 – Crow for Anyone

Holidays were always a lot of fun. It was a great time to swap some good stories and add a few more to our family quilt.

It was Thanksgiving again and Sarah had invited Doc Wilson and his wife to share the Ruark's Thanksgiving dinner. Johnny was Lee's only magnificent son who was able to come for dinner this time. And he brought his new wife, Frances, with him. Lee's other two boys Roy and Elmer had planed to spend this Thanksgiving with their new wives and their families in Baltimore. When the good eating was finished, Johnny said he had a great story about his wife Frances to share with everyone. She weakly protested but he couldn't be stopped. All of the family knew he was still a truck driver. When everyone got comfortable he began his holiday story.

"After we were married Frances used to ride the roads with me. I guess she figured if she rode with me she'd be able to keep her eye on me and I'd be a lot less likely to get in some kind of trouble. When I had a long haul delivering my produce she got to see many different places and meet a lot of interesting people. She finally got her courage up and asked me if I'd teach her how to drive my truck. I reasoned my truck was bought, paid for, and had good insurance. So if she wrecked it I could just buy another one. I began to let her drive on the return trip back home when my truck was empty. Then if we did have an accident there would be no produce to be damaged. Frances really surprised me. She took to driving my large truck like a duck takes to water. She never even scraped a fender or jumped a curb when making a turn. Her starts and stops were smooth as silk. Her parking skills were excellent. We practiced on Sundays at the large Acme grocery store parking lot across from the city park in Salisbury. All the stores in Salisbury were closed on Sundays then because of the Sunday Blue Laws. There was no one around to see a woman was driving.

A woman driving a truck was unheard of in those days. Today there are many women who drive their own trucks with the rights, privileges, and respect of everyone."

Frances interrupted here, "I like to think I was one of the women who opened the highways up for them."

Johnny continued, "I bragged about my female chauffeur to some of my truck driving friends. I couldn't help boasting about what a great driver she was. At the truck stops the guys would tease her by saying things things like 'Look out good buddies. There's that little lady trucker coming your way. You'd best clear the area, Ha Ha Ha!'"

Frances laughed with everyone and said, "And that's how I got my nickname, 'little lady trucker!"

Johnny laughed and went on with his story, "One day the truckers in the area had all planned to help a buddy celebrate. He would be driving his last haul and was going to retire. Everyone knew they were all going to meet at their favorite truck stop just outside Baltimore to celebrate his retirement. They knew today was a return trip for me. My truck would be empty and Frances would be driving. All the other drivers knew they were to meet there at four o'clock. But I was told to be there at five."

Frances took her husband's story away from him at this point, "When Johnny and I arrived at the truck stop both of us were surprised to see all of the other drivers had purposefully parked their trucks in a crowded zig zag pattern. The truckers were all standing outside the door at the front of the truck stop and were having a good laugh. They figured I would get out and let Johnny park the truck. Well to my surprise he gave me a big kiss and said, 'O.K., sweetie, show them what you can do!' Johnny got out of the truck and left me to do the parking!"

This was a good time for another big glass of lemonade! It was also a good time for their listeners to ask questions and make loud comments: "Come on and tell us did she wreck your truck?" "Bet you wish you hadn't put her in the driver's seat!" "I'd never let my wife get anywhere near my truck!" "My wife stays home and does the cooking!"

Johnny was a good storyteller and he slowly finished his lemonade. Then he continued his story, "Well after Frances sized up the seemingly impossible situation, she calmly shifted the truck's gears and methodically parked my big long truck as easily as if it had been a very small car. The truckers' jeers changed into cheers. As she climbed down from the truck a couple of the drivers lifted her to their shoulders and carried her into the truck stop. Every driver was cheering her loudly."

This story was remembered as the day Frances made the truckers eat crow.

Chapter 38 – A Thanksgiving Problem

Another year had passed. Tomorrow would be Thanksgiving dinner at the Ruarks again. Crops were good this year and everyone was well. They all felt they had a whole lot to be thankful for. This time Sarah had invited her preacher with his wife, and Doc Wilson with his wife to have dinner with her family. Carey with Tom and their little toddler also came. Of course Lee's three magnificent sons would be there as well with their new families. Sarah had planned all the fixings. They would have yams, mashed potatoes, peas with slick dumplings, okra and kale. There would also be carrots, lima beans and turnips. She would bake some of her famous biscuits and several pies as well.

The only thing missing was the turkey. Lee said, "No problem!" He took Betsy, his ole shotgun, down from the fireplace and went "Huntin."

Later he came in with a frown on his face and empty hands. "I guess our good neighbors shot all my turkeys out there in my woods," he muttered. His face brightened and with a loud Ruark laugh he said, "I've got an idea!" And out he went again. There was one loud shot from Lee's gun. He returned in a few minutes, gave Sarah a big hug, and told her, "Don't you worry. I've solved our problem."

Chapter 39 – The Great Pretender

At last it was the day of their big Thanksgiving dinner. Every one was seated around the table. Lee said the blessing and thanked God with a very long prayer. This was taking so long the Ruark children were getting hungry and starting to wiggle and whisper under their breath to each other. Fred leaned over and whispered in Janey's ear. She told Edna. She told Roy. He told Johnny. He told Elmer. He told Carey. Little excited glances and muffled giggling began to circle the table. "Well" said Lee with a chuckle, "It sure looks and sounds like all you children are having a real good giggling time of it. Suppose you share your joke with us grown ups. Then we can all have a laugh together."

The oldest three boys just broke down and laughed so hard they had tears running down their faces. They tried to tell what they thought was so funny but the words just would not come out before they'd start laughing harder than before.

Carey just smiled behind her napkin and Edna blurted out, "It was Fred!"

Lee, now half-laughing, turned to Fred and said, "Well young man I expect you ought to tell us what is so funny? So we can all have a good laugh."

Fred turned as red as a fresh picked tomato. Like his three older brothers he made an effort to speak. But when they broke out laughing again he couldn't help but join in with them.

"Well Janey," Lee said, "Can you tell us what Fred said was so danged funny that no one can repeat it!"

Janey was so proud her father asked her to explain. She stood up as tall as she could and in a sweet very loud six year old voice told her mother and father and all their guests, "We were all laughing about how silly Tom, our old rooster, looks sitting up there on the table with his legs stuck up in his ass pretending to be a turkey!"

No one was able to keep a straight face and everyone nearly fell out laughing. That sure was a good dinner and a happy time to remember. After dinner as everyone was leaving all of their guests complimented Sarah and Lee on their extraordinary Thanksgiving dinner and especially the turkey they had!

Chapter 40 – I Told You So

Thanksgiving was over. Christmas was here again. It seemed like the past year had just flown by. Everything at the Ruark home had been unusually quiet. There had not been one note from Fred's teacher, Mr. Edwards about any rowdy behaviors. Fred was doing his best to stay out of trouble.

Mr. Edwards, had used his bag of secret weapons. He taught his students in a much different way than Miss Rachel had done. He went much deeper into their studies with them and also showed them how much fun it could be to learn new things. He made them feel like explorers who were making many new exciting discoveries. Their lessons were often mixed with good natured laughter. Instead of being a stern critic like Miss Rachel had been Mr. Edwards always found some effort of his students to be worthy of genuine praise. In later years educational scholars called his style positive motivation and found it worked much better than criticism.

This was the first Christmas Mr. Edwards had been teaching in Salisbury. He volunteered with his wife, Lou Ann, to help his students put on the Christmas celebration. They planned every detail from the birthday invitations for parents, which his students had designed, to the Happy Birthday song to Jesus at the end. The festivities began at six o'clock in the evening. They started with the covered dish dinner. Every one brought the food they cooked best. It was a grand party where everyone acted like they were one big happy family and they gladly shared what they had. Then there were songs of praise, testifying, prayers, the preacher's sermon, the altar call, some baptizing, and the Lord's Supper with little glasses of wine and tiny crackers.

Mr. Edwards' students had written a play about Jesus being born in Bethlehem. He had given acting parts to every child in his classroom. Everyone was excited and his students told their parents it was going to be the best Christmas program ever. And it was! The costumes made the children look like real shepherds and wise men. Joseph was there too. Mary held a doll baby, who was supposed to be Jesus, wrapped in his swaddling clothes. Six year old Janey called them his swallowing clothes. Mr. Edwards' students had worked with him and painted a beautiful stable scene. Fred and three of his rascal friends were dressed as angels. When they sang it really sounded like angels singing the good news. Eight year old Fred wasn't amused at all when Janey very loudly told him he was a real pretty girl in his angel dress. But everyone else had a good laugh on Fred. His face turned crimson red and he tried to hide behind his father. Lee laughed louder than any one and whispered to Fred. "See, I told you so! She's just starting to get even with you for all of those times you teased her when she was a little one. And she ain't through with you yet. She remembers all those times you were so mean and she is just starting to pay you back for all of those tricks you played on her."

The pastor thanked Mr. Edwards for the great job he had done. "Does that mean I get to keep my job?" Everyone shouted in positive agreement! "Well then," he laughed, "let's give your children and my wife, Lou Ann, a big round of applause for the great job they did too!"

This was followed by a lot of hand clapping and cheering, and then home to wait for Santa Claus's visit.

Chapter 41 – A Rich Girlfriend

A favorite story this Christmas at the Ruark family home was about Elmer and his rich girl friend. Johnny started it by asking, "Elmer, remember your rich girl friend you almost married?" Roy would chime in, "Wasn't she from Baltimore?" His father's contribution was usually, "Oh I remember you talking about her. The picture you had of her showed she was real pretty too!" Fred, not wanting to miss out embarrassing his oldest brother, shouted gleefully. "I remember! Her name was Mae Belle!" Elmer loved to gamble on anything, horses, cards, what ever. He was a flashy dresser and drove one of those new fancy Ford cars with the rumble seat in the back. Once a week he'd drive to Baltimore for a big stakes card game.

He met Mae Belle on one of these trips and couldn't resist her. She was not only beautiful but a good talker and she could hold her liquor good as any man. His card playing friends told him she was very rich. Elmer and Mae began to spend a lot of time together.

Roy baited his brother further by adding, "She owned a lot of property too!"

The joke was on Elmer but he pushed his chair away from the table and began his story. "Yea!" he started, "Several times Mae casually mentioned something about all those properties she owned. She complained it was a chore keeping up with her tenants and collecting all their rent money. After one of our card games she asked me if I would drive her around to collect her rents. We made eight stops. I waited in the car while she tended to her business. At a couple of the houses no one came to the door. She explained she could get their rent the next day when she collected from her other tenants. Then she asked if I would mind driving her to the bank. She hated to carry all her cash around in her purse. I sat in the bank's lobby and waited while she deposited her money. I watched closely as she handed a large bulging envelope to the bank teller. He counted it out and wrote up a receipt for her. That sure was a big stack of money! I wanted to impress her too! I wasn't going to let her think she had more property or money than me. Back in the car she heaved a big sigh of relief and said she felt a lot safer knowing her money was locked up in a bank. I told her I always deposited most of my income in the bank too so I wouldn't lose it. Mae said the only way I'd lose my money would be in a sure thing gamble."

The family and guests always urged Elmer on. He would continue with a hearty laugh, "Well then I got an idea in my head and told her my sister was getting married on that day and I had promised I'd drop in for a few minutes. Mae quickly said she'd like to drive down to Salisbury with me. She wanted to meet my family. As we were heading down to the shore I showed her a few properties which supposedly belonged to me. I saw a well kept dairy farm with a white fence all around it and I told her when I turned twenty one my father gave me a start by putting this piece of his property in my name. I explained I wasn't much good as a dairy farmer with cows and such so I rented it out. I drove on and casually pointed to a real pretty house with a beautiful lawn and a whole lot of flowers. I told her I had bought this with my gambling winnings and my dairy farm rent. I explained it was too big for me with no wife or children. I was just renting it out until I settled down and got married."

One of the Ruark's dinner guests, Doc Wilson, interrupted, "Watch out, Elmer! You're getting in deep!"

Elmer continued, "Mae laughed and said she didn't see me getting married any time soon. I just chuckled and said it could be any day. I hoped I'd met the girl I wanted to marry if she'd have me. Seeing her broad smile, I quickly changed the subject.

"Then I saw a nice house with a couple of shutters missing

and pretended to be upset. I told her my hired man was supposed to fix and paint them two weeks before. I complained about reliable help being impossible to find. I grumbled and said I felt like selling it all, going to Florida, and starting over. Mae tried to reassure me by saying I shouldn't get discouraged because all of us property owners had our ups and downs.

"We arrived at the church in Salisbury for the wedding ceremony but no one was there. Thinking quickly I told Mae the reception was to be at my parent's house on Camden Avenue. When we drove up the lane Mae gasped, 'Elmer it looks like one of those southern plantation homes. It's just beautiful!' I couldn't resist saying, 'I thought it was a little much. But that was where I was born and raised.'"

This always caused the whole Ruark family and their guests to laugh and shout different comments such as, "Liar! Liar! Pants on Fire!" and "Elmer you should have been an actor!" and "Who Wee!" These reactions gave Elmer more fuel to finish his tale.

He continued his story, "There was a huge crowd in the yard, and the porch, and in the house. I pretended to be surprised there were so many people. So I told Mae my mother and father would be busy enough without us dropping in. She reminded me I had promised my sister. I had to think quickly and I said I could dash in just for a minute. She could wait in the car and we'd come back next weekend when there'd just be family. Mae said she did want to meet them. But she guessed I was right and said, 'Next week end would be better.'"

Everyone, including Elmer, laughed loudly at his skillful lying and narrow escape from being caught in his lies.

(This may be a good time to remind my grandchildren: it's easier and better to tell the truth in the first place than it is to get caught in a trap of lies. If you don't you'll just have to tell bigger lies to cover up your first one! This can get to be quite a tangled web!)

Elmer was nearing the end of his adventure. He went on, "I hurried across the yard, stopped on the porch for a second and chatted with a few of the guests. Then I dashed over to the newlyweds. I kissed the bride, shook hands with the groom, and apologized because I had to leave so early. I can still see their faces. Every one was confused and wondered who I was. I heard the bride ask the groom, 'Who was that stranger?' The puzzled groom answered, 'I have no idea!'"

The true story was Elmer had read in *The Daily Times* a man and a woman, both from prominent families in Salisbury, were to be married on this day and have their reception at the bride's family home.

All of his storytelling had made Elmer awfully thirsty. He paused now, pulled his chair back up to the table, and gulped down a large drink of cold lemonade.

After hearty laughs and foot stomping from everyone, Johnny jumped in and shouted, "Let me tell the funniest part! When my brother and Mae got back to her house in Baltimore all the lights were off except the one on the porch. She invited him in to have one for the road. She told him everyone would be asleep so they wouldn't be disturbed.

"As soon as she opened the door Mae's mother called down from upstairs, 'Mae did you remember to drop my house mortgage payment at the bank? I was worried about you carrying so much money of mine around in your purse.' Elmer bid Mae a hasty good night and promised to call her. Like a lot of the promises he had made before he never kept that one!"

(This story must have been at one of those dinners Edna was talking about when she said everyone's laughter, feet stomping, and loud talking seemed to cause the glass in their windows to really rattle. But this was what the Ruarks referred to as "the good ole days!")

Chapter 42 – A Fair Fight

I think one of my favorite family stories was one Lee told on his boys. Once a year Mr. Kingston let a traveling fair set up their tents on a big empty field he owned just outside of Salisbury. It wasn't because he was generous though. Lee said Mr. Kingston was a farmer and also a good business man. He charged more for the use of his empty field than he got from the crops he harvested from it. Anyway the fair was something everyone enjoyed. There were a lot of rides which were great fun. Edna liked the merry-go-round the best. Lee said it was too tame for Janey. She liked something more exciting. She loved the high ferris wheel. Each ride cost a dime. But if you paid four dimes you could ride all night until they closed down. Fred would search out a shooting game and try to win a comic book for a prize. He was a very good shooter too!

Lee's three oldest boys always came home to visit when the fair came to town. They were still working for Mr. Baxter and had their own money. There were all kinds of delicious foods sold at the fair and they bought Edna, Fred, and Janey whatever they wanted to eat. Everyone, including Sarah and Lee filled up on hot dogs, popcorn, candied apples, and cotton candy. Of course they had to have one or two of those famous fried oyster sandwiches! It was great fun but most of the Ruarks were always groaning about their full stomachs on the way home.

The fairs were some thing like our carnivals are today. The people who worked there were called barkers. There were lots of games you could play. If you won a game the barker gave you a prize. Johnny won a toy gun and holster and gave it to young Fred. Roy was lucky too. He gave Janey a little stuffed teddy bear. Elmer tried to win a prize for Edna. He couldn't win anything no matter how many games he tried. "Bunch of crooks!" he muttered.

His mood abruptly changed. "I've got an idea!" he said

excitedly. He told Edna to take Janey back to their parents and tell them he'd bring Fred home later. He and his three brothers headed straight for a tent filled with loud cheering men. There was a barker standing in front of the entrance to the tent. He was yelling really loud, "Come on in! Stay one round and win five dollars!" That was a week's pay in those days! First you had to pay a quarter to get into the tent. The big spender, Elmer, bought four twenty-five cent tickets and they went in to watch. There were two men fighting in a big circle with a rope fence around it. Elmer explained to Fred how this game was played. "You have to pay another dollar to fight the fair man who was in the ring. If you are still standing at the end of a round when they ring a loud gong you will win five dollars." Fred thought that sounded fair.

Elmer, Johnny and Roy put their heads together and did some whispering. The challenger inside the ring held his hand out for his dollar and Elmer paid him for Johnny to try his luck. Roy stayed inside to watch Johnny fight the man in the ring. Elmer led Fred quickly out to the back of the tent. They could clearly see the shadows of Johnny and the man he had to fight on the back side of the canvas tent. Johnny's shadow was tall and thin. His challenger's shadow was short and fat. Elmer cautioned Fred to be completely silent. He picked up a large heavy rock and held it in his hand and he watched the fat and the thin shadows on the back side of the tent. Fred heard Johnny yell, "I've gotcha NOW!"

When Elmer heard, "NOW!" he brought his rock down quick and hard on the head of the fair's fighter. The gong sounded loud and clear. The cheering inside the tent increased to a roar. Elmer grabbed Fred and ran for his car. He practically threw Fred in on the passenger side. He quickly started the car and raced to the front of the tent. Johnny and Roy jumped on the running boards and they were on their way home! Later at home when they were telling Lee what happened, Sarah said they should be ashamed. "Those fair men really weren't fair at all. But two wrongs don't make it right!"

Lee loved to tell this part and many years later he explained to me what had actually happened. "Those crooked men had their scheme all planned. There was actually three cheats on their side. First there was the barker who enticed you to go and try your luck. The second was the fighter inside the ring who was to work the fight around to the side of the tent. There was a third fair man standing outside on the side of the tent. He was to watch for their shadows and listen intently for his fighter inside to shout, "Ha Ha I've got you!" when he heard the "Got you!" he was supposed to knock his challenger unconscious with a big rock. The gong would sound and the crowd would drag the challenger outside to sleep it off."

Lee laughed loudly and continued, "Well it didn't go just the way they planned. They didn't realize it don't pay to mess with us Ruarks! My boys made up their own way to play their game! Elmer had changed the rules. He told Johnny to work the fight around to the back of the tent.

When Elmer heard Johnny's "Now!" he turned that cheating fair man's lights out with the big rock he had ready. Roy went with Johnny to get his five dollars. The barker who was holding the money put up a squawk. He didn't want to pay Johnny. The crowd began to get ugly and started yelling, "Give him his money!" "He earned it." "He won!" "It was a fair fight!"

Roy got their money. He and Johnny dashed out of the tent to Elmer, their chauffeur, who brought them home real fast!"

(I figured it must take a crook to catch a crook at his game. I still wondered why they called it a fair if everything was so unfair. Maybe that's the reason why the word fair was changed to carnival.)

Chapter 43 – Strange Christmas Gifts

Another Christmas and church was over as usual just past midnight on December 24. After the whole congregation sang "Happy Birthday" to Jesus everyone returned to their homes. Tonight Santa was supposed to come to the homes of the children who had been really good this year. Most of the children tried to stay awake hoping to get a peek at this funny old fat man. They were always unsuccessful because Mr. Sandman always came first. He would fill their eyes with dream sand and they would fall fast asleep.

Times were a lot different in those olden days. There was no such thing as Transformers, action figures, or electronic toys for boys. An exceptionally good boy might be lucky enough to get a whistle made from a willow branch or maybe a little hand carved sail boat or even a baseball. Once in a while a very special good girl might get a tiny set of dishes or a little homemade doll or maybe a pretty Sunday dress.

When Santa came he would put a special treat in each stocking hung on the fireplace mantle in their home. The children always woke up before the rooster crowed in the morning. They'd run to the mantle to see what goodies Santa had left for them. Most every child would be thrilled to find some special pieces of candy and maybe an orange or two and possibly an apple in their stocking. Terrible to say, but true, a really bad child would sometimes find just a strong willow switch or a piece of coal in the toe of their stocking.

Chapter 44 – Don't Spoil It

Another year had passed and Thanksgiving was over. It was again the night before Christmas. There were only three of the Ruark children still at home. They were all sleeping sound and didn't hear their mother fussing with their father about spoiling them, spending too much, and wasting good money.

Sarah said, "Lee you have been acting like your money was burning a hole in your pocket."

He really didn't feel like arguing with her tonight. He was in a really great mood. His farm and his timber cutting had brought him some extra good money in this past year. His answer to Sarah's fussing was, "Oh Muley, don't spoil it for me. This is the first Christmas I've been able to do this for my children. Money is made to be earned and to be spent. When I have it I want to buy my loved ones the best I can to make them happy. When I don't have it I just do without and with no griping!"

Sarah interrupted, "Folks round here will be thinking you are just a poor man acting like a rich man so you can have a lot of rich friends. When your money runs out you won't have as many friends. You should remember what our good book says, 'A fool will soon be parted from his money.' Remember too the old saying, 'Waste not! Want not!'"

They both turned over and pretended to fall asleep.

Chapter 45 - A Christmas to Remember

This Christmas was one Fred would vividly remember even after he was a grown man. Their new rooster crowed loudly and woke every one up! This particular Christmas all three of the children still in Lee's home found their stockings filled with treats. There was also some walnuts and a funny little nutcracker for each of them.

Under their Christmas tree Edna was happy to find two new aprons and her father had carved a beautiful small pine box for her to hold a lot of her mother's favorite recipes. There was also a lovely wedding quilt which her mother had put in the new hope chest her father had also made. She was filling it up for her wedding day set for April coming up. Robert Pottle had bought her basket at the last church social.

Janey got a beautiful porcelain doll. She named her doll Prissy. It looked so real you could almost see her breathe. She looked just like a princess because she was wearing such a fine dress. She even wore a little pair of leather shoes to take off and put back on. And she had a coat to wear if it was cold. She also had a real night gown to wear to bed at night. The best thing of all was she had the most beautiful hair. It was just like Janey's, long, dark, and curly. Janey brushed it carefully before going to sleep. Fred got an Indian chief's war bonnet, and an Indian tomahawk, and his first pocketknife just like his father's.

Everyone thought this was the best Christmas they ever had!

Chapter 46 - Back to Normal

Christmas was over. The next day was back to a normal day on the farm. It was a normal day until Sarah and Lee both heard the most ungodly horrendous scream! It was coming from the back yard and it sounded like Janey! Dropping everything they both ran to see what was happening. Janey was clutching her doll and screaming at the top of her lungs. There stood Fred holding his tomahawk with one hand high in the air. The other hand was waving what looked like a small animal or a huge hunk of hair.

Sarah covered her eyes and screamed, "Oh, dear God! He's cut Janey's hair off! Is she bleeding?"

"No," Lee answered. "She ain't but Prissy sure is a mess!"

Fred had been pretending to be an Indian with his new tomahawk. In the excitement he got carried away and scalped Prissy! She was completely bald!

Lee picked up Janey and carried her crying into the kitchen. Silently Sarah followed him dragging Fred by his hair and arm. He was pushed down onto a chair at the table. Looking mad as a wet hen Sarah plopped down in her rocker. Lee put Janey gently into her lap. She was a much better comforter than he was. Lee walked out onto the porch. He needed to cool down a bit before he spoke to Fred.

When Lee came back in Fred was still sitting silently in the chair where Sarah had put him. Janey had continued sobbing more softly now than before. After looking sternly at Fred, Lee spoke, "Just get to your room! I don't want to hear anything you might have to say. Don't you even bother coming down to supper either!"

It was a long long time before Lee even spoke to Fred again. He totally ignored him. Sarah made a little lace bonnet for Prissy. Janey, Edna, and Sarah just pretended Prissy had got a bad fever which caused her hair to fall out. She always wore her bonnet even when she went to sleep with Janey.

Nothing was ever mentioned again about the scalping. But the next Christmas Fred was very quiet. He did not seem at all surprised when he looked in his Christmas stocking and found nothing but a stout willow switch and a large piece of coal!

Chapter 47 – The Flu of 1917

The winter of 1917 should have been the time of year for people to be out sledding and ice-skating. Children should have been building snow forts and having furious but fun snowball battles. It was the time to fall down in the snow and make snow angels and also eat some delicious homemade snow cream. People ought to be visiting and gathering around the piano singing joyful songs, eating hearty meals, and enjoying the beautiful winter weather.

But this was not to be. 1917 would be remembered for years as the worst winter anyone living on the Eastern Shore had ever known. It seemed every family in the area had at least one person in bed sick with the influenza bug. There was a large black wreath hanging on most every door to warn others some one inside was doing battle with this catastrophic illness which threatened every one with the fear of almost certain death. It was a sorry time. Salisbury became famous in the Daily Times headlines because of this epidemic.

News reports regarding this horrible sickness in the United States showed a deadly parallel with the Black Death plague in Europe. Many people believed some of the young men returning from fighting World War I across the ocean had brought this dreadful illness home with them. Although it brought no consolation, this flu outbreak was not only in and around Salisbury. It was reported to be nationwide. No one had ever thought a flu season would bring as much misery as this one. All churches, schools, and theaters were closed. Public gatherings were prohibited. No one visited anyone. There was nobody strolling down the deserted streets. It was a sad and frightening time. Every precaution was taken by the local health authorities to stop the spread of this deadly sickness. In an effort to stop the flu from spreading all large funerals were outlawed because public health officials were afraid for people to meet in large groups. Unfortunately these precautions were taken with little success.

A large number of medical personnel in Salisbury had entered the military service. The ones who remained in practice here on the shore were often on duty twenty four hours a day. Even then they were unable to provide medical services to all those in need. Salisbury had a small hospital given to Salisbury by Dr. Todd. It was not large enough to care for those who were taken seriously ill because of this plague. The Jackson Memorial Building on North Division and Broad Streets was utilized as an Emergency Relief Depot. Medical remedies were also in extremely short supply. Some homes had whole families come down with the fever. Too many were dying too fast. Lee feared at least one person in every home might lose their battle.

In and around Salisbury those who reported the flu as the cause of illness numbered around 1,281. Of those there were 54 reported deaths. In an effort to prevent the disease from spreading the deceased were quickly buried to prevent the sickness from spreading. It was believed several of these cases were never officially reported. Like all catastrophic emergences many people had to care for their own family members who were fighting this often fatal disease. For various reasons they could not afford to pay for or get the medical help needed.

Chapter 48 – Old Doc's Helper

Times were so bad Lee's old friend, Doc Wilson, frequently asked him to sign the necessary forms as a witness on the death certificate required by the health authorities. Lee felt very nervous about doing this. He feared some people might claim their loved one was not dead but was buried while in a coma. After the epidemic had passed some families moved their loved one's remains to a different cemetery to be in their family plot. Some relatives claimed the deceased person's clothes had been ripped to shreds and they would be in a position very different from when they were buried. When some of the caskets were opened there were also reports the bodies inside had their hair pulled out and clutched between their fingers. Many people believed these horror tales. There were others though who took them to be untrue stories and used just to frighten people. A few unscrupulous people wanted to use these tales to claim some quick and easy money in a lawsuit. No honest lawyer even considered presenting such claims in a court of law. I suppose there was a remote possibility this kind of thing might have happened then. Today we have an embalming process to avoid the chance this would ever happen again.

Doc Wilson tried to put Lee's mind at ease by showing him how he held a mirror in front of a deceased person's mouth and nose before he declared the person to be dead. If there was no moisture on the mirror there was no doubt about it. This person was definitely deceased. After this explanation Lee, with a clear conscience, would sign the death certificate as a witness when his friend requested it.

If there was moisture on the mirror the patient would not be dead. He or she could just be in a coma. In this case nothing much could be done except to wait for the patient to regain consciousness. A surviving family member would continue to try and break the fever. The patient would either get better or die from starvation or dehydration. When this happened Doc Wilson would return and use his mirror to test for life signs again. If there was no tell tale moisture on his mirror this time he would write up a death certificate which Lee would then sign. Lee was often asked to quickly build a plain pine box for a deceased neighbor. He said one of the saddest times in his life was the day he buried his best friend Seth Parker.

As bad as things were the children seemed to adapt much better than the adults. They loved jumping rope while chanting rhymes they had made up. Someone made a rhyme about influenza. After the rhyme they continued jumping and counting until they missed the next jump and then it was someone else's turn.

"I looked out of the window!
And what did I see?
I saw a pretty bird sitting in a tree.
I looked up at him and he looked down at me.
I named him Ensah.
I opened the window and in flew Ensah!"

When Lee heard a bunch of children laughing, jumping rope, and repeating their rhyme he totally lost his usual good nature. He charged right into their group, grabbed their rope and began screaming, "Shut the hell up! Get to your danged houses, get on your knees and pray God doesn't let you get this damn flu!"

Needless to say every child there scattered quickly to their homes and that was the last of that awful rhyme!

Chapter 49 – Lee's Flu Prevention

Neither Sarah nor Lee ever admitted to having a real argument during their long marriage. But they did have some serious discussions. Their most serious one was getting the answer to the question of what was the best way to protect their family from this dreaded flu. Lee had considered all the facts and finally came up with the perfect solution. At least he thought it was the perfect solution.

Lee first rationalized alcohol was the best germ fighter there was. Doc Wilson even agreed with him on this. His second line of reasoning followed. Good Irish whiskey was nearly 98 proof. Those two facts lead him to decide on his good ole Johnny Walker whiskey!

He figured a full glass daily for each adult should do the trick. Children, like Fred and Edna, would get half a glass of the same medicine. Janey would get four small spoons full in her cup of milk. He would also tell Tom to take the adult dose, give the same to Carey, and Baby Thomas could have two small spoons of it.

Chapter 50 – Sarah's Rebellion

Rational or not poor Sarah Ruark just about lost her self control when she heard Lee's utterly absurd solution to keep his family from coming down with the dreaded flu. She began her long over due outburst with, "Lee Bahnum Ruark, you've taken leave of your senses! I've gone along with you peaceably all these years and I have always bowed down to your authority. I'm telling you now and telling you loud and clear no child of mine is ever going to take any of that ole Devil's brew you and your three magnificent sons have taken such a real liking to!"

She ranted on and on without any interruption from Lee. "Any fool with any sense at all knows whiskey is Satan's most useful tool. He has used it to lead many a good man down his slippery road to hell. So you best hear me and you best understand me now! There is no way on this earth you will ever get Satan's sinful mess past my lips or the lips of Edna, Fred, or Janey!"

When she stopped to take a breath, Lee spoke very quietly, "Well, Sarah, you've spoken your piece and I respect how you fear for the children. You've expressed yourself very loud and very clear. Now you listen to me! These children are ours together and as the head of this family I'm saying no child of mine will die from this damned plague without me fighting ole Satan himself the best I know how and that is with his own weapon, whiskey! To be sure my decision is carried out, I'll personally give our children their medicine every morning before I go out to work!"

"But Lee," Sarah interrupted in a more gentle tone.

Lee shouted, "End of discussion!" as he stormed out slamming the door behind him.

Chapter 51 – Came the Dawn

The next morning everyone lined up to take their medicine from Lee. Sarah did not! She stayed in bed until after he was gone.

All four of Lee's boys scrambled out of the house just in case there would be another discussion like last night. Fred, who could be very sensitive at times, thought his mother was really feeling poorly because of his father's decision. But the older three boys went out softly chuckling. They all burst out laughing loudly once they got far enough away from the house so they wouldn't be heard.

"Sure wish she had come out!" said Elmer.

Johnny, who was just about broke up with laughter, said "I wish he had turned her over his knee and made her take her medicine!"

"I don't know how that bird would fly!" Roy giggled. "Ole Sarah's got a lot of spirit when she gets mad!"

They all agreed with Roy.

Everyone, except Sarah, continued to take their medicine from Lee every morning. In fact Elmer, Johnny, Roy, and Lee would often drink two glasses if they were feeling poorly. Lee also made sure Edna and Fred had their half a glass. He put Janey's small dose into her cup of milk and waited to see she had finished it. Lee put the whiskey bottle in his pocket because he was suspicious of what Fred might do if he took a real liking to it like his oldest three sons had done. Lee thought to himself, *"Besides, it's mighty cold working outside all day. A little sip now and then might help to warm my insides!"*

Chapter 52 – Two Heads Together

In his own way Lee loved Sarah and he wanted to protect her from this deadly sickness. He knew she would never give in if they just butted their heads together like two old goats. He had learned early in their marriage just how stubborn she could be. Usually she never argued but she would just clam up and go about in silence.

In fact that's how he came to give her the pet name he used to call her. Whenever they had a discussion and he didn't really mind giving in he would just laugh and say, "All right Muley you can have your way this time!" and they'd just go on about their business. This time though he felt deciding on the best medicine to stop this Flu was too serious for him to give in to her. He thought to himself, *"I remember an old saying about 'two heads are better than one even if one is a cabbage head'. So maybe if Doc Wilson and I get our two heads together we can come up with a good solution to my problem with Sarah. Yeah, maybe old Doc can help me persuade her to do what I know is for the best!"*

The next day after giving out his daily ration of Johnny Walker medicine to his family Lee quickly fed and watered his animals. Then he took a shortcut through the woods to Doc Wilson's and stopped in to have a chat with his old friend. Lee was glad Mrs. Wilson was out shopping. He didn't want her to tell Sarah he had come to ask advice from his friend. Lee explained to Doc his problem with trying to get Sarah to agree with his plan to keep her well with his Johnny Walker whiskey. He concluded, "It can't do any harm. It might help fight those influenza bugs because it has so much alcohol in it."

Lee was taken totally by surprise when he heard Doc Wilson's loud laughter as he said, "Lee this is just a little scary. We are both beginning to think alike. You've come to the same conclusion I came to week before last. I went to a medical convention at John's Hopkins's Hospital in Baltimore. Like you I was beginning to worry about my wife getting sick. She would have an occasional low fever and was starting to tell me she was feeling badly. When I came home I told her a little fib. I told her a doctor at the convention had suggested I give her the exact medicine you are giving to your family. One lie always leads to another one. So I had to tell her a doctor there told me this special medicine had really helped his whole family. She has tried it and is thrilled with the results. No more complaints!"

Lee and Doc Wilson agreed on a plan together and swore never to tell their wives or any one else this secret flu remedy. Doc ended their discussion by telling Lee, "Now you just act like you know nothing. Be dumb as grass when she and I visit you all on Sunday."

Lee laughed, "That'll be easy for me! I know how to be dumb real good!"

When Lee left Doc Wilson's and went to work at the saw mill, his spirits were much higher and he even whistled as though he had not a care in the world. His happy mood was contagious and soon the other loggers were working the best they had in recent months. They all had a real good day cutting timber. Lee laughed aloud and thought to himself, *"Well this has been a profitable day in many ways. I'm sure glad Ole Doc agrees with my plan. Yep, I'll just be dumb as grass Sunday when he comes to visit."*

Chapter 53 – Silent Sunday

It was really lonely since the flu came creeping into their town. No one visited anyone because there was still a terrible fear of getting the flu from someone else. It was Sunday but all the churches were closed. There really wasn't much to do.

Both Lee and Sarah had finished their necessary work for the day. Lee had taken care of feeding his animals. Sarah finished reading her Sunday bible verses. After they finished their breakfast of left over biscuits and molasses the children gulped down their milk and hurried outside. They'd have no school today and no work of any kind. Sarah and Lee had not been very talkative since their discussion about Lee giving the children liquor as a medicine. Sarah pretended to be reading the scriptures. Lee sat busy with his fiddle trying to coax out a lively new tune. They were both surprised to see Doc Wilson and his wife ride up in their new surrey. Sarah snatched her Sunday apron off its peg, fastened it around her hips, and went out to greet them. Doc Wilson said he and his wife had been out riding in their surrey and they thought it would be nice to stop in for a short visit. Mrs. Wilson laughed and said Doc knew Sarah did all her cooking and baking on Saturday for Sunday. He had spotted Sarah's pear pie cooling on the window ledge. His real reason for the visit was to get a slice or two of it. After the pie eating with fresh brewed coffee and some welcomed conversation, Lee and Doc Wilson walked down to the barn to smoke so the ladies wouldn't be annoyed with the odor of their pipe tobacco.

Chapter 54 - Magic Medicine

As soon as the men were gone the ladies quickly caught up on the local gossip. When they finished Mrs. Wilson was bursting to tell Sarah about a new medicine suggested by a doctor friend to her husband. She had brought her bottle in her purse to show Sarah. It was very impressive with a fancy label on it and the precise instructions on how much and how often it should be taken. Mrs. Wilson confided to Sarah she had been sick with worry and was afraid she might be getting the flu. She had become terribly short tempered, and was feeling so tired all the time. She also had a serious nagging cough and sometimes even a slight fever. Her husband went to a medical convention in Baltimore a couple of weeks ago. He was discussing her symptoms with a friend of his, Dr. Hastings, who suggested a miracle medicine for her. Mrs. Wilson could not sing the praises of this medicine long enough or loud enough. She said now she felt like a new woman with so much energy! "Oh Sarah I feel like a younger happier person. It's just like magic!" she laughed.

The symptoms her friend was describing sounded the way Sarah had been feeling lately. She said ,"I don't like to complain but I have been feeling so poorly lately I can hardly get out of the bed in the morning. I feel so bad I'm getting down right cranky with Lee! Do you think your husband would be willing to prescribe this same medicine for me?"

"It wouldn't hurt to ask him," Mrs. Wilson answered. "I am pretty sure he will. I heard him bragging to our neighbors about how much it had done for me. We'll ask him when he comes in from the barn!"

Chapter 55 – Doc's Prescription

Doc Wilson returned from the barn and as he entered the room he laughed loudly, "Well, have you ladies caught up on all the important gossip and news?"

"Dear, you know I never gossip!" his wife answered with a smile. "But I do want to talk seriously with you now. Sarah has been telling me about how poorly she's been feeling and I wonder if you could prescribe some of the great medicine you got for me at the convention?"

"What's this?" laughed Doc Wilson. "I didn't know I married a female doctor who prescribes medicine without a medical license! You should go out and rest on the porch for a minute, dearest, and let me talk with Sarah before we go prescribing anything for her."

After examining Sarah and discussing her symptoms Doc Wilson decided this new medicine would cure her ailments and make her feel a lot better. He just happened to have a couple of extra bottles out in his surrey and he went out and got one for Sarah. He told her Lee was busy resolving a quarrel the children were having. But he said Lee could pay him later whenever he came to town. Sarah insisted on paying him with the money she had saved from selling her hen eggs last week. She asked him not to tell Lee she had got the medicine from him. She didn't want to discuss her health problems with Lee. Doc Wilson said he would not breathe a word of it to any one. He told Sarah to add four large tablespoons of the new medicine into a cup of warm lemon tea once in the morning and once at bed time. The lemon tea would help disguise the bitter taste of the medicine. He warned her to keep it out of the children's reach. He also reminded her not to drink it straight from a spoon because it was very strong and unpleasant without the warm lemon tea.

Chapter 56 – Ruark Survivors

It was hard for their neighbors to believe the Ruarks had all survived this worst winter flu epidemic. None of the old timers could remember one like this in their lifetime. Everyone in the Ruark family had to take Lee's remedy. Sarah secretly took Doc Wilson's prescription. And no one in their family came down with the deadly flu.

(I wonder now was it luck or coincidence or was it a real cure?)

Neither Doc Wilson nor Lee ever breathed a word about how they got their wives to take the "medicine" Lee had suggested. Doc Wilson and Lee both agreed it was worth a try and it didn't do any harm.

For some reason the whole Ruark family showed the most pleasant dispositions during this winter season. There was a lot of laughter, joking and singing as well. There was even some whistling from all when Lee was not around.

Thank God! It was finally spring! All the crocus Sarah had planted were pushing their heads above the ground in spite of the thin layer of snow trying to tell the lie it was still winter.

The danger of spreading the flu no longer existed. Once again it would be business as usual. Bans were lifted on large gatherings now. Sarah was really happy she would again be able to have her family dinners on holidays and the Lord's days.

Chapter 57 - Miss Sprocket

Another year had passed. Poor Sarah was really over burdened and still worrying about everybody. She felt responsible for everyone and everything. She always tried, usually unsuccessfully, to keep the peace between all the members of her family. She used to whisper her prayers daily. Now they had become audible and loud. Lee began to wonder if she was becoming peculiar like Miss Sprocket who lived in Salisbury.

Almost everyone in the town felt sorry for Miss Sprocket. They were very patient and kind when she stopped anyone she saw on the street. She would always say with great happiness in her voice, "Tomorrow is Sunday. Rodney will be here and we will be married. Oh, I can hardly wait! I'm so excited! Of course we want you to come to the wedding. It will be at 3:00 o'clock. And don't forget to come and bring your family too!"

Poor thing! It was really pathetic. The truth was Rodney had been a real scoundrel and left her waiting at the church five years ago. On that heartbreaking Sunday she ran home sobbing, and crying, "I wish I was dead!" She wore her tattered wedding dress and tied a lot of beautiful ribbons in her hair until the day she died.

The meanest boys in Salisbury had made up a horrible rhyme to torment Miss Sprocket with. They used to follow her around chanting loudly:

"Poor Miss Sprocket lost her pocket.
There's nothing in it! Nothing in it!
Just the ribbons round it!"

Miss Sprocket's parents had taken her to see many specialists who all said she had suffered a severe nervous breakdown. There was nothing they could do for her. They recommended everyone should speak kindly to her and just let her enjoy her fantasy of Rodney coming to marry her. Everyone knew he never would.

Chapter 58 – Lee Lost His Patience

Lee was usually a pretty patient man with Sarah. But her peculiar behavior was becoming very annoying to him. It was really beginning to get on his nerves. Finally one night at dinner, he totally lost it and shouted out, "For God's sake and for my sake Sarah will you please shut the hell up? You'll drive me crazy if you keep up this infernal jabbering!"

She looked at him so strangely, calmly set the bowl of mashed potatoes on the table, and walked out of the room. Lee ignored her behavior, picked up the bowl of potatoes, put a nice large helping on his plate, and passed the bowl to Fred. Now Fred didn't say anything but he thought this was very odd behavior from his parents.

After finishing his meal Lee went out on the porch, slammed the screen door, and sat down on the swing. He tried to think and see if he had done anything wrong. *"No. I've been acting just like I always do."* He took a pinch of his snuff and rolled it around in his mouth for a few minutes. When it was ready he spit a glob of the juice from his mouth off of the porch. Well, not quite! It landed on the porch railing. "Damn!" he muttered and took another good pinch of snuff from the can he carried in his shirt pocket. He stuck it way back into the side of his mouth. He leaned back, put his feet up on the railing and tried to relax.

The house was so quiet. Even Janey didn't whine like she usually did when she was sleepy at the end of the day. Fred, very gently, picked her up and carried her into his parent's bedroom. He put her into her bed and covered her up with her nice warm quilt. It would get cold after the old wood stove went out for the night. He saw his mother just sitting by the window. She was muttering something but he couldn't understand what she was saying. Without speaking he slipped silently from the room and up into the loft where his feather bed was lying on the floor. Sarah had often said she wished he could get a real bed. But he told her not to worry. He liked it and could pretend he was camping out. Tonight he really wished he could be out camping in the woods.

    Edna put the supper dishes ever so quietly in the dish basin to soak over night. She cleared the table and put the leftover food in the ice box. Then she went quickly to bed and pulled her quilt up over her head. She stayed awake and silently worried most of the night. *"Why did this have to happen now?"* Carey was expecting a little Mumford baby any day. She had asked her father to let her come and stay for a short while to help her. In the morning Lee assured her they could manage a few days without her. She reluctantly climbed into the surrey with Tom and they raced away to his house where Carey waited nervously.

Chapter 59 – Silent Sunday

After Lee and Sarah's one-sided quarrel it remained deathly silent in the Ruark home. Sarah stayed in her room and gazed out the window. Lee got up in the morning tended his animals and then went to work to cut some timber. When he came home at night he made supper for Fred, Janey, and himself. They all three ate in silence. Lee went out to sit in his porch rocker and tried to think. After putting Janey in her bed Fred crawled wearily under his quilt and covered up his head. He had a hard day taking care of his mother and Janey and he was bone tired.

The next morning was the same. Lee got up, tended his animals, and went to work at his logging job. When he got home at night he again made supper for himself and the two children. Like the night before they all ate in silence. Fred again put Janey and himself to bed. Lee went out to his porch rocker to do some more thinking.

Chapter 60 – Fred Goes Missing

Lee was wishing to himself, *"Edna would be such a big help taking care of Janey and Sarah while I'm at work. It's not likely because Carey needs her to help with the delivery of their baby. There isn't anyone else I could ask. I'll just have to rely on Fred keeping watch over Sarah and Janey. He isn't much to depend on. To be fair though he is only nine and he did volunteer to do his best to help me with them so I could keep my extra job as a logger."*

Things went along fairly well for a week. Then one night Lee came home to find little Janey, now seven years old, crying at the top of her lungs. She was really dirty and crying like she was starving. Fred was no where to be found. Sarah was still sitting gazing out the window. After much struggling Lee finally got Janey in some clean clothes. Feeling a real sense of accomplishment he heated up some left over food and fed her. Then he held her in his arms in his rocker by the fire and tried to comfort her as best he could. He was a bit awkward but he talked easy to her like he did when he was trying to calm one of his animals. After she had been changed into clean clothes, got her belly full, and was being held securely in her father's arms by the warm fire Janey was content. She cuddled down and fell fast asleep. When Lee was sure she was sound asleep he tucked her gently into her bed under her quilt to keep her comfortable. Then with fire in his eyes he went to find Fred! It took him quite a spell to bring him out. The tone Lee was using to call him scared Fred almost to death. He knew he would be killed for sure if he came out. But he knew his death would even be worse if his father had to hunt him down. Lee heard a very scared little voice coming from the outhouse. "I'm in here! I'm scared to come out! I know you're going to kill me for sure. I'm sorry. I really am. I just couldn't make Janey stop crying and I didn't know what to do! Please don't kill me!" Lee laughed with relief. He had been so fearful and certain some gypsies had stolen his son and carried him away. "Get yourself out here so I can hug your scrawny neck. I'm not interested in killing you at least not until you tell me all about your exciting day!" A very timid Fred ran into his father's arms. They walked together holding hands all the way to the house. Lee fixed them some supper. Then they sat by the warm fire and Lee was given a full report from Fred. Lee sort of apologized to Fred for giving him such a big responsibility. He promised he would find a better solution and make arrangements for some one older to watch over Sarah and Janey when he had to go to work. Fred was so relieved he would no longer have to take care of his mother or his baby sister. He volunteered to clean out the horse's pound, gather up the chicken's eggs, wash down the hog troughs, and even milk the cows for Lee. "Well Fred, you are taking on a mighty big work load for being just nine years old. But I'll bet you can do most of those jobs. I think I've made a real good bargain with you here tonight." laughed Lee. "Now let's get to bed because tomorrow is going to be a busy day for all of us!"

The Ruarks weren't much for displays of affection but tonight Fred put his arms around Lee and said, "Good night and thank you for not killing me! I love you!" Lee put his arms awkwardly around Fred, gave him a hug, and answered, "I love you too boy!"

(Years later my Uncle Fred told me this was the only time his father ever said he loved his boy.)

Chapter 61 – Lee's Promise

After Fred went up to his loft Lee went in and tried to talk softly to Sarah and figure out what they should do. When ever he would ask her a question or for her opinion she would just respond with some gibberish which made no sense to him. Lee was not a man who worried a lot. He believed, 'Worrying was like a rocking chair. It just keeps you busy but it never gets you any where.'

He was a very logical man and could always find an answer to any problem he came across. This time was different though. At first he thought Sarah might be hungry. However she just would not eat or drink anything he brought in to her. Thinking she was just overly tired he tried to put her to bed. Sarah was much smaller than Lee but when he tried to put her gown on and lay her down she fought him with the strength of three men. So he just kissed her forehead tenderly and whispered, "You know I truly love you Muley, and we'll figure this out together somehow, I promise you." Then he left the room quietly. Sarah still sat by her window staring out at the night sky.

Chapter 62 – Doc Wilson's Advice

Morning always came early on the farm. Lee did not have to get up this morning. He had stayed up all night sitting on the front porch trying to figure things out. When the sun came up he fed his animals first while he was trying to decide what he should do for his beloved Sarah. Not being able to get any answers by himself he decided to go see Doc Wilson. He hoped to get some help in understanding what was happening with Sarah and why she was acting so peculiar. More importantly he needed a wiser man like his friend to help him decide what should be done to help his beloved Sarah.

He hitched up his buckboard and then went in and bundled up Fred and Janey in their quilts to keep them warm on the chilly ride to town. Sarah had fallen asleep in her rocker and he thought it would be best to just let her sleep until he returned from his visit with Doc Wilson.

Doc Wilson and Lee were very close friends. But he was never one to sugar coat anything serious. After Lee explained about Sarah's peculiar behaviors Doc Wilson spoke to him in a kind but direct manner. He told Lee he was a good general doctor for broken bones and delivering babies. He admitted he didn't know much about what was troubling Sarah. He was afraid she might be suffering a mental breakdown like Miss Sprocket. "No! No! Not my Sarah!" Lee wailed with tears gushing from his eyes and pouring down his cheeks.

Doc Wilson was finally able to calm him down. He assured Lee he believed Sarah had not completely lost it as Miss Sprocket had done. He believed she had just suffered a slight nervous breakdown due to the stress of caring for so many children and her bad habit of worrying so much about things she could not control.

Doc Wilson reminded Lee, Dr. Todd had donated his home on Locust Street to the town of Salisbury to be used for a hospital. A lot of remodeling had quickly changed his old house into a suitable place to treat sick people. An excellent doctor was there and also some of the very latest equipment and techniques. Later it became known as Peninsula General Hospital.

Lee's friend convinced him it was urgent to take Sarah first thing in the morning to the new hospital. He also said the sooner Sarah got treatment the more certain were her chances of recovery. He reminded Lee how Miss Sprocket's family had put off going to the doctors until two years after her traumatic experience.

Mrs. Wilson had been watching the children while Lee and her husband were talking. Like a good doctor's wife, she had taken Fred and Janey into the kitchen for some breakfast. She didn't want them to hear the details of their mother's condition. She had also listened and overheard Lee's problem with Sarah. She volunteered to care for the two children until Lee got back from taking Sarah to see the doctors. She and Doc Wilson both told Lee not to worry about his children. If he needed to stay with Sarah a while they would be just fine with them. Lee thanked them both and said he would bring some clothes and food for his children when he and Sarah came by early the next morning.

Chapter 63 – Terribly Afraid

When Lee got home he quickly gave Fred and Janey a couple of warmed up biscuits with molasses and a cup of milk. When they had finished he sent them off to bed. Sarah was still sitting in her rocking chair. It was starting to get dark and she had not even lit their kerosene lamp. He lit the lamp, patted her shoulder awkwardly, and pulled her shawl up around her back.

Then laughing to hide his worry and sadness he said, "Hey there Mrs. Ruark how about if I fix us some supper tonight?"

Sarah just stared at him with vacant eyes as though he was not really there. He sat down on the floor next to her chair and gently lowered her down to sit beside him. Sarah looked up at him with tears flowing from her eyes and whispered, "Oh Lee, I'm so sorry! I'm terribly afraid I'm losing my pocket!"

Lee knew what she meant because in those days people referred to your head as your pocket. They said your head was a pocket which carried your brain around. Anyone with mental problems was said to be losing their pocket.

Lee wrapped her tenderly in his arms and said, "Don't you worry dear Sarah we'll find it together. I promise you!" They sat there through the night waiting silently for the sun to rise.

Chapter 64 – Two Good Friends

The sun was not up yet. The early morning air was quite chilly. Lee wrapped Janey and Fred up in their quilts and lifted them up into his buckboard. As usual Fred started complaining. Janey was wide eyed and very quiet. She was only seven but she was very bright. She had always liked a routine and knowing what was coming next. She didn't like this one bit.

This morning Lee had explained their mother was real sick and needed to go to the hospital. He said the doctors there could make her well again. Lee was not accustomed to explaining any of his actions in the past to anyone and especially not to his children. He did his best to put their minds at ease because he was getting agitated with their whining and asking questions he did not have the answers for.

After he got them settled as comfortably as possible he went back into the house. He led Sarah out and gently seated her up beside him on his buckboard's front seat. Lee was talking very soft and coaxing to her. "Yes Sarah it'll sure be nice for the four of us to be taking a trip to town. I think we really ought to do more visiting now the boys are grown and gone."

Fred and Janey looked at each other. They were young but they were not fools. They knew their mother must be awfully sick or he wouldn't be treating her so nice and easy. Sarah never spoke. She just sang softly over and over the hymn she used to sing to Afrey.

Lee lectured the two children all the way into town and he told them he was going to leave them with Doc and Mrs. Wilson while he was taking their mother to the hospital. He threatened to whip the daylights out of them when he got back if they weren't good. This really scared both of them and they started to whimper.

He ordered them to stop such nonsense and told them it would really be a treat to visit with Doc and his wife. "She's the best cook in the whole town and Doc can play his fiddle almost as good as I do. Besides you might even get to ride through town in his shiny new surrey if you are really good." Hearing this Fred and Janey temporarily lost their fears and rode quietly into Salisbury.

Mrs. Wilson welcomed them with a big hug and a smile on her face. Her husband took the children's clothes and two quilts from Lee and laid them on a chair. He said to Fred, "I'll bet you'd like to play a game of checkers with me!"

His wife laughed and said, "Yes and he will most likely win too! I'll bet right now these two children would like a nice big slice of cherry pie I baked this morning. What do you say?"

Fred remembering his manners spoke up quickly, "Oh yes! Thank you mam! Pie would be mighty fine!" She took them both into her cozy kitchen which was full of the most delicious smells. Lee slipped silently out the front door.

Chapter 65 – Peninsula General Hospital

The hospital in Salisbury was very calm. The nurse who greeted him at the front desk tried to talk with Sarah but got no response. She asked Lee a few questions and wrote his answers on a required form. Then she told him they would have to keep Sarah over night in order to run some tests to determine the cause of her problem and decide the best treatment for her. Without waiting for him to agree or not the nurse gently led Sarah into another room in the hospital.

Lee hadn't expected this. He thought in his heart they would just give Sarah some medicine and then he could take her back home. Now though he knew in his head the doctors would be the ones calling the shots. If he wanted his Sarah to get better he would have to let her stay. He went out to have a talk with Major. "I can't see no sense in you taking me back home and coming back in the morning. It'll be too far from here to get a little sleep. Then I'd have to come two more miles back here tomorrow to see what these doctors have to say. I could sleep in my buckboard while you haul me around. But I think it'll be too hard on you old friend!"

He decided to go downtown and get a few supplies he needed on the farm. After this he left Major tethered on the street near the hospital and took a long slow walk around to collect his thoughts. He had no success at figuring anything out. He softly moaned, "Oh Sarah, it's just beyond me why something like this happened to us."

It was starting to get dark now and Lee decided to sleep in his buckboard. First though he wrapped his nice warm horse blanket snugly across Major. Then with a long sigh he climbed into the back of his wagon and wrapped up in the quilts he had wrapped Sarah in this morning. After snuggling down he said his prayers which ended with a reverent prayer for his dearest Sarah. Closing his eyes he silently thought, *"I'm right here*

Sarah. It's sure been a long day. But we need to remember, 'This is the day our Lord has made. We will rejoice and be glad in it!' We both know it was the Devil brought this into our home but we also know the Lord will give us strength to overcome it!"

It had been a long day and it was an even longer night for Lee.

Chapter 66 – A Referral

It seemed to Lee the sun was rising very slowly this morning. He hurried up the steps when he saw the nurse unlock the hospital door and put a sign in the window. They were finally open. Lee began to anxiously question the nurse.

She told Lee the doctors had decided he should take Sarah to the hospital over in Cambridge. She gave him a paper for the Cambridge doctors which explained what the Salisbury doctors had decided. She assured Lee the Cambridge doctors had special training and experience to successfully treat patients like Sarah.

The nurse had explained to Sarah she would be taking a short trip with Lee. She was ready to go. When Lee came into her room he was thrilled to hear her say, "Wait until I get my hat!" It was the first normal thing he had heard her say in a long time. Smiling broadly he helped her up to sit beside him on his buckboard seat. Lee hollered as he cracked the reins, "O.K. Major, Giddy Up! We're going to get my Sarah well!"

It was a long ride to Cambridge. Again Sarah had become silent. Lee tried to make it a pleasant ride. He chattered until he was tired of hearing his own voice. Finally he gave up and resigned himself to a long silent ride.

Chapter 67 – Sarah's Diagnoses

When Lee saw the Cambridge hospital in the distance he felt a strong sense of relief. Sarah's silent behavior convinced him he could not make her well. It would be up to these special doctors.

Major stopped at the front door as though he knew what he was supposed to do without Lee telling him. Sarah seemed very tired from the long ride and Lee helped her up the steps. As they entered the front hall Lee noticed it was very peaceful and people appeared to know what they were doing.

A nurse in a crisp white uniform welcomed them, and asked for some information which she wrote down. When they finished she told Lee to read and sign it if she had got it all down correctly. Lee could barely read and he never let anyone know he hadn't finished the fourth grade in school. So he just pretended to read it and said, "Yup, it looks good to me." He scratched his name at the bottom of the page.

The nurse tried to talk to Sarah but she was not responsive. Then she told Lee they would have to keep his wife overnight because they would have to do some tests, blood work, and maybe even take some pictures of Sarah's brain. Lee interrupted her, "That ain't even possible!"

"Yes it is!" she answered. Then she went on to explain, "In 1896 a German physicist, Wilhelm Roentgen, designed a radiation machine which made it possible for doctors to actually see how damaged the brain was."

(It was first known as a Roentgen ray and is now called an X-Ray.)

It was a lot for Lee to grasp. But he understood they would have to keep his Sarah over for the tests. He told her he'd be waiting outside. If she wanted him all she had to do was tell the nurse to get him and he'd be right in. Lee kissed his Sarah gently and went out again to his buckboard. After putting a hunk of snuff between his teeth and the inside of his mouth he wrapped Major up in the warm horse blanket again. Then he laid down and wrapped up in the quilts he had used the night before. He was warm and quite comfortable. After saying his prayers he gazed up at the stars in the dark night and thought about his life with Sarah. *"It's been so good. Why did you let go Sarah? You have always been the one that held us all together. If you leave us now what will become of our family?"* There were no answers and he finally drifted off to sleep.

Lee had sort of expected to wake in the morning in his own nice warm bed at home. All this past week's nonsense would just be one of those wild dreams he sometimes had. But no, the sun came up and Lee woke up in his cold buckboard. He was right where he went to sleep last night. He felt half frozen. But his first thought was of his sweet Sarah. *"What had they found out? What'll they tell me? No sense sitting here worrying. I might as well go and see what it is, good or bad, and get it over with. That's my way. Meet something head on and be done with it."*

Chapter 68 – A Plan for Sarah

A different nurse came to meet Lee in the front hall of the hospital. She introduced herself as Nurse Banning. She seemed very nice and was very reassuring when she told Lee Mrs. Sarah had rested well and had a good nights sleep.

She explained she had been assigned to see to Mrs. Sarah's comfort if he decided to let her stay with them for a while. They walked through two large doors at the end of the long hall. In the center of the room they entered was the largest round table Lee had ever seen. There were seven chairs placed around it. Nurse Banning sat in one of the chairs and motioned for Lee to sit in the one next to her. A smiling young man sat in the chair on the other side of Lee. The nurse introduced him as Jackson and explained he would be Mrs. Sarah's attendant and escort her around outside for the first few weeks of her stay. Jackson offered to show Lee around the yard and garden later after his meeting with the doctors.

Lee was familiar with the term "gaggle of geese." What he saw made him think of a "gaggle of doctors." After counting he realized there were four of them and they appeared to be all talking at once. However they became more reserved and professional as they approached the table and took their seats. *"Phew!"* All Lee could think was, *"This'll sure cost a lot more then I've got. But I'll just get another part-time job to make it possible for my Sarah."*

One doctor named Keating did the talking. He did a lot of talking too and never seemed to get a bit out of breath. He used a lot of terms and long words Lee could not understand. He summed it all up by saying they had all examined and diagnosed Sarah's condition and agreed her problem was just a minor nervous breakdown. It was minor at the present and had been caught in time. With rest, therapy, and medication they all felt sure a complete recovery would take place. They recommended she stay in their care for at least a year. The doctors felt the really good news was Mr. Ruark would be able to take his wife home by spring for weekend visits and holidays.

All of the doctors had been smiling and shaking their heads in agreement. Lee's hope had been built up on every word Dr. Keating uttered. When he got to medication and rest Lee thought they meant Sarah could take her medicine at home and rest there too. So the part about being able to go home by Spring just for weekends and holidays really knocked the wind out of his sails. He tried bargaining with the doctors. Then like a good Irishman he even argued some. But he knew, in his heart, they were right when they said if she went back home too soon she would only get worse.

Lee thanked the doctors and went with Jackson and Nurse Banning as they showed him around and answered all of his questions. They showed him Sarah's room where she had been resting quietly. He saw the dining room where some of the patients were enjoying a good lunch. Then they all sat with Sarah in the social room until it was time for him to leave.

Saying goodbye and trying to tell Sarah what was happening was awkward for Lee. She just sat and stared off into space the same as she had done at home. Nurse Banning said it always took the patients a while to come back to reality and it was best not to try and force it. Lee knew his beloved needed to rest and he felt this was the place for her to get better. He thanked everyone for their help and kindness toward his Sarah and left quickly so as not to prolong the pain of separating.

Chapter 69 – A Good Idea

Riding on the way home Lee had a lot of time to think. He knew he did the right thing for Sarah. It sure was going to be a long lonely ride. He hated to be all alone in his empty house tonight. He knew his three boys would be out carousing somewhere. Edna was still helping her older sister, Carey. Fred and Janey would be with Doc Wilson and his wife. He reasoned to himself, *"It's getting late if I go straight home I could come back to the Wilson's for Fred and Janey in the morning. It'd be a shame to wake them all up in the middle of the night!"*

"Hell," he thought, *"To my house and back to Doc's house in Salisbury in the morning and get my younguns. Then I'll have to turn around and take them back to my house! It'll be a long ride for nothing. I might as well spend another night sleeping in my old buckboard in Doc's front yard. He won't mind. I can just pick up my younguns in the morning, tell Doc and his wife about my trip, and enjoy a good warm breakfast to boot!"*

Lee laughed out loud, "Good idea, Lee! Giddy up there Major! Just take me to Doc's house for the night!"

Chapter 70 – Thicker Than Water

With Sarah in the hospital and the doctors saying Lee should come to visit her at least once a week it became necessary to schedule her chores and some of his to the other family members. Sarah had carried a very heavy work load for so many years without complaint. "Now," Lee explained to his family, "It is someone else's turn."

Lee's children all came to his and Sarah's rescue. They had all been taught and believed "Blood is thicker than water." Throughout their lives they would always stick together when ever anyone in the Ruark family had a real problem.

Carey had given birth to baby Thomas and she was already up and about. She could watch over Janey and little Thomas too. Edna also came home to help. She was given the job of gathering the eggs and milking the cows. She was a little clumsy though. She often dropped one or two eggs and broke them. Once as she left the hen house she dropped the whole egg basket. She was a little better at milking the cows. She could get a whole bucket of milk from them. But it was half empty where it had spilled out of the bucket as she carried it to the house. Thus her chores fell to her younger brother, Fred, who was next in line. Fred grumbled constantly now. He didn't believe his sister was dumb or clumsy at all. While she sat on the porch rocking and shelling peas, peeling potatoes, or husking corn she would smile at him in such a wicked little way. Then Fred knew for sure she was neither clumsy nor dumb. She was smart enough to get out of the harder chores around the farm. Janey enjoyed watching little Tom. So Fred got stuck with the chickens and the cows and his regular chores too.

Chapter 71 – What Goes Round

Carey's husband, Tom Mumford, quietly spread the word around to all of the neighbors. He let them know about the hard times Lee and his family were having now with Sarah in the Cambridge hospital. They all talked about how Lee and Sarah had helped them through the years when they needed it especially during the dreadful flu epidemic in 1917. Sarah had often left food from her family's meals on the porches of her neighbors who were too sick to provide for themselves. They also remembered how Lee had often made a wooden pine box to bury one of their loved ones. Now they really felt sorry for Sarah and Lee. They took this opportunity to pitch in and help them in return. All of his neighbors believed the old saying, 'What goes round comes round!' Tom was a good neighbor and a big help to Lee as well. He would drop in often and pitch right in helping. All the while he just pretended to be visiting and enjoying the good cooking of Carey and Roy. The neighbors knew with Lee having to visit Sarah weekly he was having a hard time keeping his farm work caught up. Many of them came to help with his crops so he could visit Sarah regular.

Miraculously those good people were there at planting and also at harvesting time even though they had crops of their own to get done. When Lee protested they'd be quick to come back with, "Lee, that's what good neighbors are for. You and Sarah were a mighty big help to us when we needed it during the flu and we're not about to forget it neither!" This was a better lesson than any taught in school. The Ruark children learned the seeds of friendship sowed by Lee amd Sarah had come to a bountiful harvest!

Chapter 72 – Laughter Again

All three of Lee's grown boys came back home to help their father. They knew he would have to spend a lot of his time going to visit their mother. So Elmer and Johnny chose to help with the harder farm work. Roy, who didn't like farm work at all, offered to work with Carey in the kitchen. He really liked to cook and was pretty good at it. He had learned by watching his mother who was the best cook around.

He could make biscuits which were out of this world. Once they were so delicious and light they disappeared long before the rest of the meal was put on the table.

Roy asked, "Where's all the biscuits?"

Everyone laughed loudly and about fell out of their chairs.

"Well hell" answered Elmer, "They were so light they must have flown right out of that window over there!"

"Sure," answered Roy, "I've an idea they flew right into your stomachs!" More loud laughter followed.

Lee heard them all laughing and smiled as he came in from washing up at the water pump. It was good to hear. It was the first time any laughter had been heard in the Ruark home since Sarah had gone to the hospital.

Chapter 73 – Pride Before a Fall

Lee was having trouble sleeping as he lay in bed. He was so thankful he had such wonderful neighbors. Everyone knew he was a proud and independent man. Some said maybe a little too much. He thought to himself, *"Well, I've got a right to feel proud. I've worked hard all my life. I've been able to show a good profit on my crops and my timber cutting. I haven't wasted my money. I've always set a little of it aside each year. I was able to buy a couple small pieces of land joined up to my piece. The meager acre I started out with has grown into this nice sized farm I own free and clear with no mortgage or entanglements. I've been lucky enough to marry the finest lady in the whole county and she's given me a bunch of challenging children to raise. They were all able to get a good schooling if they wanted it and we all survived the flu. I've built a nice home for my family and provided for them as good as most. Now when every thing was starting to come together and looking so danged good it seems the old devil is trying to throw something bad in our path with my love getting so sick. But we'll win, Sarah. We've not come this far to get beat down. I know you'll soon be well and we'll be back up on our feet again. Just hold on tight little lady for all of us. Together we can handle anything old fool Devil throws our way. Let him give it his best shot!"*

Lee was so lost in his thoughts he had not been aware of the terrible storm working up outside until he heard a loud clap of thunder. *"Everything is secure for the night. I might as well call it a day,"* he thought as he blew out the kerosene light and crawled into his lonesome bed. He tried to get to sleep and not think too much or too long on his sweet Sarah. Lee's last thoughts were, *"The Lord knows how much I miss you, Sarah!"*

Chapter 74 – The Devil's Best Shot

Lee woke to the sound of a terrible crash and the room lit up like daybreak. The family all came scurrying into his room. Some were crying and others just hollering. Elmer looked out of the window. "Christ! The barn's on fire!" he shouted. No one stopped to notice they had nothing on but their winter long johns. They all ran out together with one thought, to save their father's barn!

Elmer, the strongest, ran to the pitcher pump and began pumping water furiously. Edna and Fred grabbed some milking buckets and pails for him to fill. Johnny and Roy ran into the blazing inferno and got all the animals safely out of the barn.

Poor old Lee just stood and gazed not able to believe what he saw. He finally realized the rain was putting more water on the blaze than they were and the fire was still burning. When he saw how useless their efforts were he shouted in exasperation, "Hell, we are just pissing in the ocean. We might as well stop! Let her burn!" He just stood there helpless with tears streaming down his face.

It was the first time any of his children had ever seen their father cry. He had always told them they should never cry unless they were hurt and in terrible pain. So they reasoned he must be hurting real bad because he was crying, a whole lot! Soaking wet and exhausted everyone followed him silently into the house to see little Janey sleeping peacefully in her bed. Lee was not one to mention God only on very rare occasions.

They were all startled to hear the silence broken by the loud outburst of his laughter. "Well, Thank God! We're really blessed! It wasn't our home or anyone in our family got burned down. It looks like the Devil did his worse and he didn't even scare my little Janey a bit! She slept right through all his ranting and raving."

Lee proudly took up his fiddle off of the wall peg and played a lively little tune.

Janey woke up and joined in with all the Ruarks who were doing a little jig dance around the room. Then everyone fell exhausted into their beds. They were relieved their father had recovered his old self again. Sinking wearily into the soft down of his quilt a very tired Lee thought to himself, *"My little Janey isn't scared of anything not even the Devil who was fierce enough to make her old Peh cry! Yes indeed, little Janey, you'll make your mark in this world someday. I wish my boys were as tough as you. I wish too you'd been a boy because you'd be quite a mess to do any kind of business with. I sure hope we can get to be partners some day."*

He laughed aloud because he heard in his mind the time Sarah had said, *"Lordy Lee, if wishes were fishes we'd have a whole bowl full!"*

Chapter 75 – Reality

The large pile of burnt wood brought everyone back to reality. It was hard to realize the huge pile of charred lumber was where Lee's barn had been. The family all learned reality is more often than not just plain hard work. Everyone rolled up their sleeves and began to dig in and try to clean up the mess. Elmer hitched up Sully, his father's mule, and brought Lee's hay wagon around. Lee, Johnny, and Roy began loading up the bigger pieces of wood. He was only eleven years old, but Fred tried to do a man's work for a change. Edna went in to make breakfast. An eager to learn nine year old Janey followed her into the kitchen. Ham, eggs, fresh made biscuits, and strong coffee would make the Ruark men work a lot better.

Before lunch a few neighbors ambled in. Without saying a word, they began lifting the heavy timbers onto their wagons to be hauled away. Lee tried to find words to thank them. They cut him off with remarks like "This is just a thank you for all the times you and Sarah helped us." Someone said, "And besides your girls are pretty good cooks and we haven't had our lunch yet."

Carey and Edna kept the food and the coffee coming. Janey enjoyed playing with little Thomas and keeping him from getting under foot. "Lee, let us know when your barn raising will be. We'll see you then!" Someone added, "And we might even stay for supper ha ha!"

Tom, Carey, and Little Thomas were the last to leave. Lee said, "Our neighbors are great people. Thank you Carey and thank you Tom."

"Well," said Tom. "You know the old saying. 'What goes around comes around!' Besides you are now a grandfather to our little Thomas and we are all family!"

Lee's boys couldn't resist some good natured teasing and called Lee "Grandfather" the rest of the night.

Chapter 76 – A Very Good Offer

It was Spring again and Sarah had now started to come home for her weekend visits and she seemed almost back to normal. She was alert enough to notice the new barn the neighbors had helped to raise. She saw it was larger and had one of those fancy lightning rods on top of it. Because she had always worried about money she asked Lee what it had cost. He told her not to start worrying again. It hadn't cost him a penny. Mr. Spencer, the young man who owned the saw mill down the road, had paid for it. He had been real impressed by the turnout of friends and neighbors who came to help Lee when his barn burned down. Talking to them he had learned about Lee's honesty, truthfulness, and dependability. He thought Lee was just the kind of man he was looking for.

A few weeks after the new barn raising Mr. Spencer came out to the Ruark farm. He and Lee talked for quiet a while out by the barn so they would not be interrupted. After they finished their conversation they came to the house for a cup of coffee and a big helping of Edna's bread pudding. They were both smiling broadly. After shaking hands Mr. Spencer said as he was leaving, "Lee, I'll see what can be arranged to benefit us both and get back with you soon."

Lee let his family wonder what was going on for a whole week. But he finally burst out with his good news. He just couldn't hold it inside any longer. Mr. Spencer had offered him the steady job of foreman at his saw mill just on the outside of Salisbury. For the first time in his life Lee would be drawing a good steady weekly salary. He would have real money in his pocket and be able to pay off the rest of Sarah's stay in the Cambridge hospital. His salary could even increase depending on how much timber he could get the other loggers to cut in a week. With the right foreman like Lee, Mr. Spencer's old saw mill could cut out a stand of timber in a really short time. Mr.

Spencer said Lee could pay so much out of his wages back to him for a specified time and then Lee could eventually own the Salisbury sawmill himself.

Mr. Spencer explained he only wanted to keep his Salisbury mill long enough to help pay for the new one he was planning to build in Pocomoke. This would be closer to where his wife's family was and she wanted him to build her a home there too. She didn't like him riding to Salisbury to work all the time. He had to leave for work before the sun was up. It was past dark before he got home at night. They had no time together except for Sundays. And now she was expecting a little one they had both agreed it would be better to have his sawmill in Pocomoke near her parents.

Hearing Lee's good news his three older boys started immediately on negative comments like, "Yeah, but remember like our mother has always said, 'Don't count your chickens before they hatch!' And another good saying she had was, 'A bird in the hand is worth more than two in the bush!'"

Lee didn't want to hear remarks like these so he just laughed and said, "Yes she did say that and I also heard her say once, 'I don't need you to rain on my parade!' This is my opportunity and I'm going to believe and enjoy it!" Well his news still sounded too good to be true to his boys. But it sure would be great if it really happened. And he was the happiest they had ever seen him. His fiddle came down from its peg for his celebration dance!

Lee didn't share all of this good news with Sarah yet. He was afraid it might be too much for her to understand for a while. The whole family promised not to say a word to her about it. But they all felt she would have to know something was going on because Lee was smiling so much. He was even whistling and singing out loud lately. It wasn't natural. But it sure was nice!

Chapter 77 – Not Good News

It was Sunday night. Sarah was much better. She had spent a whole week with her family and enjoyed it very much. She was very tired tonight though. A few of her neighbors had dropped in for a visit. It was nice to have company but she had fallen asleep in her rocker in front of their warm fireplace. Lee picked her up, laid her down in their bed, and tenderly covered her with their quilt. Then he went quietly out to his rocker on the front porch to do some more thinking. The children and Lee had been happy to have Sarah visit for a whole week. Lee hated the fact he had to take her back to the hospital in the morning. He had to though because he had promised to bring her back Monday before ten o'clock. Her visit here at home seemed so short. But he knew it was helping her to be back with her family. She was beginning to act more like she had when they first met at the church social so many years ago.

The night was as dark as the inside of a bruised crow. Lee glanced at his pocket watch. It was almost ten o'clock. He thought he saw a man's figure coming up the path. He went quickly into the kitchen, grabbed his shot gun from the wall, and returned to his rocker. He sat silently and thought to himself, *"There's nobody out this late at night up to no good! But I'll be ready for the rascal!"*

It was a man and he hollered out, "Hello there Lee! Don't shoot! It's just me your old friend who lives down the road." Lee yelled back, "Well you'd best stay there till you tell me exactly who you are and what you are doing out here on my property so late at night. My finger's getting a bit touchy on this trigger."

"Lee, it's just me Hiram Sloan. You know we've hunted many a coon and killed many a bottle of liquor together in all the year's I've known you!"

Lee shouted back to him, "Well come on up old friend. I couldn't recognize you in this dark night." To be on the safe side Lee kept his gun on the floor beside his rocker. He leaned against his porch railing. Hiram sat down in Sarah's rocker next to Lee's.

"Well what's so important you had to come and visit me this late?" Lee asked.

Hiram began, "Lee you don't really want to know."

Lee laughed and said "Then you really didn't have a reason to come out here to visit with me! You could have waited until tomorrow."

Hiram hesitated a minute or two and then he said, "Well, I bring bad news for which I'm sorry. But I thought you needed to know because you had some business dealings with Mr. Spencer."

"Come on Hiram, you know I'm not a real patient man. Just spit it out!"

"Well," Hiram said, "He's dead!"

"Oh Hiram, I know you like to play tricks on people just like my son Fred. But you shouldn't joke about something like death. Mr. Spencer is only about thirty years old. You might cause him some bad luck if you talk about him being dead!"

Hiram persisted, "I can't cause him any more bad luck. I'm telling you the truth Lee. He's dead! I heard it at Clancy's Bar in Salisbury. I didn't believe it either. So I went over to the funeral house and sure enough I saw him with my own two eyes. Dead as a door nail he was!"

As an old saying goes, the wind went right out of Lee's sails. He gasped, grabbed the porch railing and sat down quickly in his rocker. "I just can't believe it," he mumbled.

"Well it's the truth! I knew you and he were supposed to work together somehow in a business deal as soon as you both signed some kind of paper to make it all legal. Because you're my friend I tried to find out every thing I could for you. When I left the undertaker's I stopped in at Mr. Thatcher's office. You probably knew he was Spencer's lawyer. I tried to get him to tell me something but he was tight lipped as a clam and wouldn't tell me anything. While I was there Spencer's father-in-law came busting in. With all of the excitement I guess Mr. Thatcher forgot I was there. He told the father-in-law Mr. Spencer had a will. He had left everything to his wife if he should die before she did. The old man got happy as a Junebug. And said he was going to persuade his daughter to sell everything and move out to California on the west coast with him!" Here Hiram stopped for a breath.

Lee was still confused by all this horrendous news. "But I just talked to Spencer about noon today. He stopped in on his way home from church and asked me if I would go with him tomorrow morning to sign those papers. I asked him if I could wait till Tuesday because I have to take Sarah back to the hospital tomorrow as soon as the sun comes up. I just can't believe all of this. First the flu, then my barn, then Sarah, and now Spencer! What have I done to get four such bad breaks so close together? Old Devil Man must have been staying awake at nights figuring this all out. He sure has been busy messing in my business!"

Hiram made a clumsy attempt to cheer Lee up by saying, "I know how you feel, Lee. Remember though 'when God closes a window he'll open a door.' I still believe everything happens for the best. I'm sure you'll find something even better."

Lee just thought to himself, *"I can't think of anything better than me owning my own sawmill!"*

Lee didn't even go to Mr. Spencer's funeral. He couldn't tolerate everyone coming up to him and saying how sorry they all were he wasn't going to be able to have his own sawmill. He didn't bother to tell Sarah about Mr. Spencer dying either. No sense in getting her upset. Let her keep on thinking everything was working out fine for him.

Chapter 78 – Time Flies

I've heard this old saying before: "Time or tide wait for no one!"

And I guess that's what happened to the next ten years. They just seemed to fly by.

Lee's older Ruark boys had left the Ruark nest and now had their own familes. Remember Carey had married young Tom Mumford when she was sixteen. She moved into his house in Salisbury. Later on her sister, Edna, married Robert Pottle. She now had three children Robert Jr, Nina, and Norman. They lived on Short St in Salisbury. Elmer and his wife, Mary, moved up to Baltimore because she wanted to live in the big city. Their son was Maurice. Johnny was next to move out. He had built a little bungalow on Zion Road, in Salisbury and married Frances. They had a son named Jackie. Roy, the youngest of Lee's magnificent sons, moved to Delmar with his wife Grace. They had three daughters Grace, Alline, and Doris Lee. Now the only young Ruarks still at home with Sarah and Lee were Fred and Janey.

Lee was a little pleased to have his children in their own homes now. But he never showed it at any time. He had given up on trying to talk much with Fred. He was still the tricker. Giving him advice was like the wind blowing in the breeze. Fred knew he knew it all! Janey was different. She acted like she believed every word her father spoke.

Sarah still wanted her children to come back home for their family dinners. Truthfully she was getting old though she never admitted it. She was no longer able to cook all the food like she had done in previous days. But she still believed her dinners were what would hold her family close together.

So Carey and Edna planned with the wives of Lee's

magnificent sons to provide most of the food. Sarah still insisted on making her delicious pies. And Lee took turns with his boys turning the ice cream churner to finish up the meal. Thus a new plan came into being. It was also decided not to have their weekly Sunday Dinners. Instead they all agreed to have their family dinners on Thanksgiving and Christmas. This worked very well. The grandchildren enjoyed hearing the Ruark family stories. They even added a story of their own sometimes. And again you could see the windows shake when everyone was talking all at once!

Chapter 79 – Lessons From Lee

From the time Lee changed his daughter's name from Emma to Janey she grew up knowing how much her father wished she had been a boy. She knew she was his favorite child from then on. He raised her on his hope they would do well in some business venture one day. Many times she heard him bragging about her. He was certain she would go farther and do so much better than those rascally sons he and Sarah had raised.

Janey had inherited her father's smooth tongue and persuasive abilities. She also inherited his determination. She used those traits along with her good looks to try and get what she wanted in life. She paid attention to his bits of advice and learned many of his lessons early in life. "First you should set your target. Don't let anybody tell you it can't be done. And never let any one say you are just a pretty woman. Well you are but you also have a mighty big brain in your curly little head! Just never give up on your dreams!"

Chapter 80 – Importance of Choices

Janey was now grown and married to Ralph Corbin and she had moved into his house. She was expecting their first baby. Her husband, Ralph, wasn't home very much because he was interested in becoming a race car driver. This kept him on the road often to take part in some big race somewhere else. Since he was gone frequently Janey had a lot of time on her hands. She often went back to her home to visit with her parents. When she did her father always cautioned her and tried to teach her what he thought were the important things to know. Young Fred had told his father years before when Janey was just a baby she would only be capable of keeping house for a man and putting his meals on the table. And now she was just a housewife with a baby on the way. Lee still believed Janey could make her good fortune if she would make the right choices in life. She told her father Ralph was a hard working young man. But Lee never really liked her husband. "*Yes,*" Lee thought to himself, "*Ralph does work hard. But it seems like he spends too much time tinkering with his own car. He should be fixing other men's cars for the garage where he is supposed to be working. Then he could use his money to buy some property for him and his family. But it was her choice, dag nab it!*" He still silently worried. "*Had she made the right choice? But what's done is done! She'll just have to make the best of it now!*"

His dream was still for his daughter, Janey, to have it all. He wanted her to believe family was very important and to be cherished. But he had taken every opportunity to fill her head with his ideas of owning property and making sufficient money to better herself!

"Now don't take me wrong," he'd say to her. "I loved my family more than my own life. But it cost me a pretty penny to provide for all of them and they were never much help to me financially! With Ralph by your side you could do real good. You should only have one child and with two incomes you could save and invest in buying property which could provide you with more income."

Lee really believed property was the way to gain wealth and often reminded her, "Land and houses are better than money in the bank!"

He prophesied, "If you don't own your home, the banks could fail and take your house because you can't make the mortgage payments on it. Then you'd have to live in the woods like a squirrel or a rabbit!"

He almost always added, "The most important thing you have to do is make certain you make the right choices in your life. Bad or good things don't just happen to you for no reason. Every choice you make will determine the kind of life you'll have. Wrong choices will make your life bad and you miserable. Good choices will make your life a lot smoother and more enjoyable. So just remember every thing you do is a choice. But you must make sure it is the right one!"

(And now I hear myself telling this to my children, my grandchildren and my great grandchildren in different words the very same thing today!)

Chapter 81 – A Chicken in Every Pot

Herbert Hoover was President in 1929 and was now living in the White House. Times had been gradually getting bad for quite a while. Lee never called him President. He used to refer to him as "our daddy Hoover" when he was talking about him. President Hoover had won the election by promising to "put a chicken in every pot!" Lee's remark which brought the most laughs was, "Our daddy, Hoover, up there in Washington must have forgot our chicken! Now most folks don't even have a pot!"

Lee had often talked to Janey and the rest of his family about how the banks could close down any time they wanted and keep their money. Well, that's exactly what happened just like he had said in the past. He had always refused to put any money in the bank and he assured his family their money would always be safe in his good old coffee can. He'd laugh and say, "I've got it buried where no one could ever find it!" (And no one ever has!)

Just as Lee had prophesied the banks closed in 1930! Their doors were locked up tight! No one was able to get any of their money. *The Daily Times* newspaper in Salisbury had reported the terrible news from New York City. The stock market had collapsed!

Chapter 82 – The Real Depression

All of the Ruark children were now grown up. When they came home for Thanksgiving or Christmas they heard their parents talking long and serious about what had caused this Depression. In the larger cities across the bay there were many people who had shot themselves or jumped to their deaths from their office building windows. It was hard for Lee's family to understand what was happening and why anyone would do such a dreadful thing.

Lee assured them it wasn't the poor people or even the blue collar workers like him doing this. "It was just some of those stupid millionaires, bankers, investors, doctors, and those who were always living too high off the hog! They were acting so crazy because they lost all of their money. They had big mortgages on their magnificent mansions. They had a lot of bills to pay for their fancy cars, boats, and other extra stuff they didn't need. They were going to lose all of their stuff now because they couldn't pay for it. They were even afraid because they didn't know where their next meal was going to come from. Because they believed they were ruined financially they didn't think they could go on living. Well some people might think I'm dumb but I'm sure not stupid. There is nothing worth dying for except maybe my family if I had to keep them safe. We don't need all of the stuff those jumpers had. As long as we have each other we can make it through anything old man Devil throws our way!"

Because of the Depression, Lee's three boys had moved back to Lee's home with their wives and children. Edna had said, "Three more roosters have come back home to roost and they've brought their hens and biddies too!"

Elmer explained their predicament to his parents, "Well we

boys were sorry to have to come back here and live off of you again. But Mr. Baxter wasn't able to get any of his money out of the bank and he couldn't afford to pay us any more. There wasn't much money and no jobs anywhere. People were going out of business and closing up their stores."

Sarah spoke up, "Well I feel sorrier for those Yankee women then I do for their men! A few of those city ladies had maybe saved a little change. If they went to a store to buy a loaf of bread there wasn't any on the shelves. Poor dears they didn't have sense enough to know you can make biscuits with a little bit of flour, a couple spoons of lard, and some water. They could have used some of their flour and browned it in a pan, added a little water and had some tasty gravy to pour on their biscuits."

Lee interrupted, "That's true enough Sarah but they probably didn't even have any lard or flour. And they had most likely never been taught how to make do like we do."

Sarah cut him off with, "Those people up north must not have had much teaching at all or they'd know what our good book teaches us. Every one in our family knows the worst sin of all is to kill yourself. I believe that is the only unforgivable sin and if you do it you can't ever expect to get into Heaven!"

Probably for the first time in their lives all of the young Ruarks were really listening to their parents vent their frustrations. Johnny laughed and said, "You can really preach it because you sure are telling the absolute truth!"

Lee wasn't finished and he continued on, "Yeah when those city fools thought they had lost ever thing they should have just hitched up their britches and started over again. There isn't any one here on the eastern shore going to starve. We've got our hogs that provide us with lard, pork chops, bacon, sausage, and scrapple. Our goats, chickens, and cows, give us meat, eggs and milk. I can always find a little bit of work some where and trade the pennies I make for some flour and…"

Again Sarah jumped in, "And if every thing runs out we can all just go picking and get some peaches, strawberries, blueberries or tea berries and I can make you some fruit cobblers to make you forget you were ever hungry!"

Everyone whooped and hollered at the idea of Sarah's cobblers. Johnny said, "All this talk about food is making me hungry."

Roy jumped up and said to his mother, "I'll get the dishes out! Your cobbler over on the table looks mighty tasty!" Even in such scary times the Ruarks found their family was a true blessing.

Chapter 83 – Time for Sarah

Sarah had been home for quite a while now. Fred was with her and Lee. But he was still the tricker and didn't spend much time at home. He did come home to eat, sleep, and get his mother to wash his clothes. Her three grown sons had returned to their homes with their own families. Edna and Carey survived the depression with their husbands in their homes. Janie had married Ralph Corbin and they lived in his house in Salisbury. Their first baby, Violetta, was now a year old.

Sarah didn't have much to keep her busy and she mostly sat in her rocker during the days. It did worry Lee a little because she had developed a habit of muttering quietly to herself. He tried to console himself by thinking she was probably just praying or learning some new verses from her Bible.

In the past if Sarah needed guidance or just another grown person she could talk with, she had a few neighbors. She lost some of her closest friends because of the terrible flu in 1917. Her church had burned to the ground while she was in the Cambridge hospital. The church leaders decided not to rebuild. They moved into Salisbury and built a new modern church. Most of the people she had been friends with had either died or moved away.

When she was a patient at the hospital in Cambridge she had someone called a counselor to talk with. He said the main reason for her breakdown was she kept all of her problems inside and was never able to talk about them. Even though she was home now she felt she was slipping back into her old ways. She had given serious thought to what her counselor had told her. It seemed everyone in the family was so busy they didn't have any time to visit with her. Lee was always busy outside. She was so lonesome. There wasn't much for her to do. Now the children were all grown she couldn't find anything to keep herself busy.

Lee had been acting like he was walking on eggs. He had kept his temper under control. He was always agreeable with her and never did anything he feared might get her upset. She told Lee they needed to have a serious discussion. He was puzzled by her strange request. He wanted to keep her happy though. So he quickly agreed to another friendly discussion. A little smile came to her lips as she remembered their early years of marriage and their lively dish cuss shuns.

Chapter 84 – A Serious Discussion

Her smile quickly faded and she spoke in a serious tone, "Lee, I'm afraid you won't like this talk very much." She began by telling him they had shared a good marriage and had raised a pretty fair bunch of children from their time together. She felt her whole life had always been for and about him and his family. It had never been about her and what she wanted or needed.

"Now Lee," she said, "it's got to be my time for a little while. I have to have some peace and quiet. I have to be able to do something I need to do or just plain feel like doing." It was hard to explain but she knew she had to do this. She wanted Lee to understand why she was so troubled. She told him she was afraid she was slipping back into her old ways. She had too much spare time on her hands. This frightened her more than anything. She did not ever want to go back to the Cambridge hospital again!

With tears in her eyes she continued, "I'm terribly afraid to stay here any longer, Lee. I can't get the thoughts of our dear boy, Afrey, out of my head and my heart."

He started to speak but she kept on, "I know our precious Afrey isn't here on this earth. He died too soon and we all miss him. I know he is in Heaven now. But I'm beginning to believe he is here in our house listening and talking to me. I have to tell you I've started talking to him a lot lately. I want to be with him so bad. I'm right ashamed to say it but I've been tempted to finish my life here on earth. I know that would be the most awful thing of all. We both know our Good Book teaches we shouldn't do anything to hasten to leave this earth until God calls us home with a natural death. I know if I was to end my own life I would have no hope of ever getting into Heaven.

Then for sure I'd never see our precious Afrey, again."

She continued, "You've told me a hundred times you couldn't tolerate living in town. So I think it'd be best if I just move into Salisbury for a short spell. It would just be long enough to make sure my mind is going to stay right. I need to be close to a church I can attend regular. I need to pray and ask the Lord to protect me and make these feelings and dreadful thoughts go away."

Lee felt he had been dealt a deadly blow. He had listened to his beloved Sarah in silence. Now he felt he was surely going to die. He gave a long sigh which seemed to draw all the air out of his body and his brain. He was completely confused. Lee loved Sarah more than he loved his own life. He was never one to talk about his true feelings. He had been looking forward to his life with his precious Sarah after their children were all grown and gone. He sat in silence and thought on this. It seemed like an eternity to Sarah.

At last he spoke, "Well Sarah, I sure don't understand most of what you are telling me. Our family has stuck together through all the bad times. Now our children are grown I was thinking we could spend the rest of our lives together until the Lord takes us home. We can relax now and spend the good times we have left together."

Sarah interrupted, "Lee, my mind is made up. I wish I could make you see how bad I feel about this. I don't rightly understand it myself. But I just know it's what I have to do now. Hopefully after I get my mind right I'll be able to come back here to live again with you if you'll still have me."

"I see your mind is made up, Sarah. But I don't want any talking about nonsense like that. You'll always have a home here anytime you want it. If you are set on leaving I'll do my best to try to understand. There is one thing though. There won't ever be us talking about any divorcing! I meant what I said, 'For better or worse till death do we part!'"

"I figured that's what you'd say. I meant it too when I said, I'd love and obey you till death do we part. I really don't want a divorce either! I just feel a separation for a short time will be the best thing for both of us."

"Well, I can see there isn't any need trying to make you feel any different. Fred is grown but still here at home so I expect it'll be best to let him stay here with me. I just don't think you'd be able to deal with his mischief which he's not out grown yet."

"That's fine with me. Lee, I hope you can try to understand how mixed up I am. We shouldn't get into any argument. If it's all right with you I'll plan on leaving in the morning."

"Sarah you must know how much I love you. I guess I haven't told you as often as I should. I know you are a wise woman. You wouldn't do any thing this drastic if you didn't know it's the best for you. I'm not going to argue and try to change your mind. We'll try it your way, just for a little while."

There was a long pause. He was crying silently. Tears were pouring from his eyes and running down his cheeks. He went on, "Please don't say it's none of my business and forgive me for worrying about you. But I'm just wondering have you planned ahead? Do you have a place to go? Will you at least let me take you in town with your things? I want you to stay so bad. But I reckon you know how you feel and what you need."

Sarah answered, "Just for a short spell I'll be with Edna. I know how you feel and I care about you. I know how you must be a hurting because I'm hurting too. But I have to think about myself for a while. I would appreciate it though if you could take me into town in the morning."

Lee quickly answered, "Sarah, you know I'll do anything you want. All you have to do is ask me." This conversation was followed by another long awkward pause.

Lee broke the silence by saying, "Well you best be getting to bed and get rested up. You've got lots to do in the morning. I'll go check on my animals and do some front porch thinking before I turn in."

Chapter 85 – A Trip to Edna's

Sarah had got up as usual before the rooster crowed. She got the fire going in the kitchen stove to warm up the house. Sadly she thought to herself, *"Reckon I won't be doing this anymore. Maybe Fred'll do it for Lee. God, I need a sign to tell me this is the right thing for me to be doing!"* There was no sign from God. She only heard the rooster crowing and Lee giving his usual cough as he stepped off the porch to go and feed his animals. Lee hitched up to his buckboard and stayed in the barn as long as he could.

When he finally came into the house Sarah poured him a cup of coffee which he drank slowly. He was standing close by the stove silently hoping she had changed her mind. She silently pointed to her things beside the door. He picked up her one suitcase and one box she had waiting.

He mumbled "Sarah, are you sure?"

She interrupted, "Yes, Lee," and walked out to the buckboard. They rode in complete silence into town. When they pulled up to Edna's house she was waiting on the front porch. Sarah hugged her and walked inside. Lee put Sarah's suitcase and box down and turned to leave.

Edna hugged him and whispered "Oh, I'm so sorry!"

Lee turned away, wiped his eyes, and softly said, "It's for the best for my Sarah." Then with a deep sigh he stumbled down the porch steps and climbed into his buckboard. His faithful friend Major carried him back to his empty house now filled with so many memories.

(Some were bad but most were good!)

To Be Continued...

www.ingramcontent.com/pod-product-compliance
Lightning Source LLC
Chambersburg PA
CBHW080403170426
43193CB00016B/2797